GOD IS NEVER LATE;
He's Seldom Early; He's Always Right On Time

by Stan Toler

BEACON HILL PRESS
OF KANSAS CITY

Copyright 2004
Beacon Hill Press of Kansas City

ISBN 978-0-8341-2105-8

Library of Congress Cataloging-in-Publication Data

Toler, Stan.
 God's never late, He's seldom early, He's always right on time / by Stan Toler.
   p. cm.
 ISBN 0-8341-2105-0 (pbk.)
 1. Christian life—Anecdotes. 2. Christian life—Meditations. 3. Christian life—Humor. I. Title.

 BV4501.3.T65 2004
 248.4—dc22

                                                    2003025796

20 19 18 17 16 15 14 13

Dedication

To Deloris Leonard on the occasion of her retirement after 34 years in the Trinity Church of the Nazarene office. No one has worked harder and stayed longer in order to see God's work accomplished. Your loyalty, encouragement, and support are deeply appreciated.

Special Thanks

To Jerry Brecheisen, Jeff Dunn, Mark Hollingsworth, Deloris Leonard, and Pat Diamond for editorial assistance and creative consultation. And to Bonnie Perry, Barry Russell, Judi Perry, and all my friends at Beacon Hill Press. It's a pleasure to partner with each one of you in ministry.

Contents

Introduction

The resident of an assisted living home got off the courtesy van and walked directly to the dining room, in time to get his favorite table.

"Where have you been?" his buddy asked.

"Been to the ear doctor," the man replied.

His buddy teased, "What for? To get an estimate?"

"No," the man replied, "I got me a brand-new hearing aid—the best money can buy!"

"No kidding!" the dinner buddy responded. "What kind?"

With a puzzled look, the man answered, "What time? Oh I don't know. I think we left about 9:30."

Forgive that new twist on an old groaner. But time and events can be a little confusing—even some of your own time and events. We desperately want to have control over time, making things we want to happen occur when we want them to. When we were kids we wanted to open our Christmas presents on Christmas Eve eve. We couldn't wait for our schooling to end so we could get started in "real life." Now, we want to take early retirement, because we can't wait to "stop working and start living."

And when it comes to our relationship with God, we seem to be in different time zones altogether.

God seems to have delayed His presence.

Maybe He's on a well-deserved break.

Does heaven have a lunchtime?

Maybe you feel like you picked one of those numbers in the

bureau of motor vehicle line and there are 78 others still ahead of you. But you need God to wait on you—right away.

This book is about some of those feelings. It's about your best and worst times. It's about trusting God even when it seems He is running late.

It's about God's perfect control over the times and events of our lives—and about His perfect power to order those events in a loving and meaningful way.

This is the third in a series of books about life and God's mighty working power in the midst of it (*God Has Never Failed Me, but He's Sure Scared Me to Death a Few Times* and *The Buzzards Are Circling, but God's Not Finished with Me Yet* are the first two). *God Is Never Late, He's Seldom Early, He's Always Right on Time* is about your appointment with our God. And you can be sure He'll never be late for it. You may delay in coming to Him (or even making the appointment in the first place), but God will always be there.

I pray that the positive mesage of this book will encourage you to trust Him—even when you can't see Him; to call on Him, even when you're not sure He is listening—and to trust Him, as if your very life depended on Him. And by the way, it does!

Do What You Can, and
God Will Do the Rest
(Little Is Much When God Is in It)

Maybe you've heard about the preacher who forgot to take his sermon notes to the pulpit. Either he was running overtime and spied his wife on the second row pointing to the Timex on her wrist, or he knew the pastoral vote was to be taken following the service, but in the midst of the sermon he got some truth turned around. Flustered, he said, "The Lord took 5,000 barley loaves and 2,000 fishes, fed five people and had plenty left over."

An unruly parishioner near the front of the little chapel spoke up loud enough for everyone to hear, "Anybody could do that."

"Could you?" asked the minister, unaware that he had the numbers mixed up.

"Certainly."

After the service the minister complained about the man's

conduct to one of his board members. As the board member gently pointed out the error, the preacher thought to himself, "Well, next week, I'll fix that fella."

Sure enough, the next week the preacher looked carefully at his notes on the podium and confidently began the second sermon of his series. And once again, he brought up the miracle of the loaves and fishes. He told how the five barley loaves and the two fishes had fed the multitude of more than *5,000* people. Then he pointed to the heckler and asked emphatically, "Now could you do that?"

"Of course," said the heckler.

"And may I ask how?" the frustrated minister replied.

"With all that food you left on the platform from last Sunday."

It's one of the great incidents in Scripture. After the miraculous healing of a crippled man and the assault and battery of some religious skeptics, Jesus and the disciples regrouped.

"Jesus crossed to the far shore of the Sea of Galilee (that is, the Sea of Tiberias), and a great crowd of people followed him because they saw the miraculous signs he had performed on the sick. Then Jesus went up on a mountainside and sat down with his disciples. The Jewish Passover Feast was near" (John 6:1-4). Suddenly the crowd grew. Dramatically it grew. And soon the hillside was filled with people hungry for something more than religious traditions.

They wanted a miracle in their hearts.

Feeding 5,000 from a boy's sack lunch was just as easy for Jesus as creating moons or mountains. Someone once said, "Miracles are the common currency of heaven. The feeding of the multitude was just a little loose change spilling from a hole in its pocket." Although the New Testament is filled with miracles, the feeding of the 5,000 was one of such magnitude that it is recorded in all four Gospels. Let's take a look at this incredible—and true—story of God's amazing grace.

Why? Because you and I need miracles from time to time. You may not be called on to feed 5,000 (unless you have a big family and they're all dropping by for lunch after church). But you and I come face-to-face with uncertainties—financial, physical, social, or spiritual—that need God-answers. We need to know that He has enough to make up the slack. We need to know that He cares enough about our condition to give us more than a passing smile or a heavenly nod.

We need to grasp the words and deeds of a proactive Lord. We need to see Him move through the obstacles of our lives with power and purpose. The clocks of time are moving at breakneck speed, and we need to understand that they are not without a power source. (Though sometimes it looks like the batteries are not included.)

But here's the deal: God has your situation under control.

He doesn't need any subcontractors. And He doesn't outsource. He simply gives you an invitation to take baby steps of faith toward His inexhaustible and eternal supply.

MIRACLES OFTEN START SMALL

I'm reminded of the little boy who wanted $100 very badly. He prayed for two weeks but nothing happened. Then he decided to write God a letter requesting $100.

When the postal authorities received the letter to GOD, U.S.A., they decided to send it to the president. The president was so impressed, touched, and amused that he instructed his secretary to send the boy $5. The president thought it would appear to be a lot of money to the child.

15

The little boy was delighted with the $5 and immediately sat down to write a thank-You note to God that read: "Dear God, Thank You very much for sending me the money. However, I noticed that for some reason You had to send it through Washington, D.C., and, as usual, they deducted $95."

Like all great works of God, the miracle on the mountainside started simply. It began in a Judean kitchen with a rustic knife, some warm bread, and a couple of fish so freshly caught they were still trying to do push-ups on the kitchen table. A little boy and his mother were up early that morning, packing a lunch so he could go to the big gathering his friends had told him about. This "Jesus" person, whoever He was, always drew a big crowd. And like any curious little boy, wherever the crowd was, that's where he wanted to go. His mother reluctantly agreed, concerned about her son's journey and the large crowd.

She, too, had heard about Jesus. His teachings had amazed the religious leaders. And His miracles made the headlines in the local newspapers. Perhaps she was too busy or had too many other family responsibilities to go herself, but she didn't want her son to miss out on a life-changing moment.

Her son didn't need any coaxing.

With a small boy wonder over such a big event, he pulled on his hand-me-down tunic, laced up his sandals (the ones without the Velcro), and draped a small bag over his shoulder—the bag full of loaves and fish. I noticed that his mother gave him five smaller loaves, rather than one large loaf. You know how little boys are. If she had given him just one, he would have opened that shoulder bag at about nine o'clock and would have eaten the whole thing in one sitting! (And then he probably would have cooked him up some fish sticks on one of those roadside barbecue grills.) So she gave him five individual loaves. Knowing moms, she probably told him not to eat them all at once too.

He had no idea how big this day would be.

Come to think of it, that's always true of the day when one meets Jesus. Until you actually meet Him and let Him pour His miraculous life into yours, you have no idea how marvelous the experience can be.

This lad couldn't have understood that this would be the day when he would walk into the pages of history. He didn't know that of all Jesus' miracles, this would be the only one that all four of the Gospel writers would feel compelled to include in their accounts of Christ's life.

And certainly he didn't know that he would experience one of the great principles of Christian living. Later, when he would offer his lunch to this "Jesus," he would learn the lesson of a lifetime, one that every seeker after truth must understand: *Receiving is a by-product of giving.*

For several hours that day, this small boy carried five loaves and two fish in his shoulder bag, completely unaware that every person he met, and thousands beyond his sight, would benefit from its contents.

If it's true that you have to *give in order to live*—and it is—he was about to live in a big way.

Understanding God's *possibility* and *proximity* begins with your personal and inner commitment to give something of yourself (even if it's the tiniest step of faith) as a down payment on receiving from Him. Now don't get me wrong. There's nothing you or I can do to "earn" God's favor. We can't afford grace, no matter how many credit cards we have. And He has committed himself to our situation, period.

But throughout biblical history, He has offered people an opportunity to "share in the miracle." For example, to blind Bartimaeus, He queried, "What do you want me to do for you?"

His response to the question resulted in his sight. To the centurion, who longed for the healing of his dying servant, Jesus ordered an immediate journey back home (without a miracle in hand). The miracle was in the journey, however. His faith was part of the dynamic that resulted in the healing of the servant. He has given us the privilege of seeing our commitments, small as they may be, rewarded by His unlimited supply.

And often, those commitments are born in times of calamity or uncertainty. That's when we pull on our hand-me-downs, lace up our spiritual sandals, pack up whatever provisions we have, and run to meet Him.

EVERY MIRACLE BEGINS WITH A PROBLEM

"When Jesus looked up and saw a great crowd coming toward him, he said to Philip, 'Where shall we buy bread for these people to eat?' He asked this only to test him, for he already had in mind what he was going to do. Philip answered him, 'Eight months' wages would not buy enough bread for each one to have a bite!'" (John 6:5-7).

Berneele Daniels tells the classic story of a young child who went to his father and said, "Dad, are people really made of dust, like the Bible says?"

"Yes," the father replied curiously.

"And we're all going to return to dust when our bodies die?"

"Certainly, why do you ask?"

"Well, I was looking under my bed and I saw somebody either coming or going."

Have you ever been in a place where you didn't know whether you were coming or going? A situation arises, and suddenly the pages in your daily planner turn to concrete. The problem brings everything to a standstill. And the solution seems to be harder to find than real silverware at a church supper.

Philip, the disciple of Jesus, was in that kind of predicament. He had at least 5,000 people gathered on a wilderness hillside—without a Burger King in sight—and he was in charge of the refreshments. It was getting late. Everybody was getting hungry. (And you know how cranky religious folk get when they're hungry.) The service was long, and the air-conditioning was out. Some were even ready to faint from the heat (and maybe from the hunger). They needed refreshment *now*. What was he going to do?

Jesus saw the problem (He always does, you know) and asked Philip where they might get some food for this big crowd. Why? It was one of those "faith questions." Jesus knew that Philip had the analytical mind of an accountant. He was sizing up the situation in human terms, and he was stretching for a human solution. But Jesus wanted to help him see something bigger than spreadsheets, bottom-line balances, or pizza deliveries. Jesus already had a plan in mind—and the disciple was part of the plan.

Philip's response was true to form. He quickly pointed out that eight months' wages wouldn't feed that bunch. And, Philip was undoubtedly thinking of *his own* wages.

Philip gathered the other disciples and took the typical High Church approach to solving problems: They formed a study committee. One cynic said that a committee is a group of people who individually can do nothing and collectively decide that nothing can be done. That's a predictable response when faced with a gigantic problem—describe how impossible it is. But every miracle begins with an impossible problem. If you don't have a problem, you don't need a miracle. However, if you do have a problem—good news—you're a qualified candidate for a heavenly solution.

EVERY PROBLEM HAS A SOLUTION

Did you hear the story about the game warden who spies a redneck walking up the bank from a pond with a bucket of fish and asks to see his fishing license?

"Don't need one," the fella replies. "These is pet fish."

"What do you mean, pet fish?" the game warden demands.

"I keep these here fish in my bathtub at home as pets and bring them here once a week to swim with their old buddies and then I load them back up and take 'em home after their visit."

"What kind of fool do you take me for?" cries the game warden. "Them aren't pet fish, you just caught them today."

"No siree, these here is pet fish," the redneck insists.

"Prove it," yells the game warden. "Let me see them do one of them visits you was talking about."

"All right, sir, you just watch here," and the ol' boy sets the bucket in the water.

The fish quickly swim off and the game warden says, "And how long do you expect me to sit here and wait for them fish to finish their so-called visit?"

The redneck asked, "What fish?" (Source unknown; received via e-mail)

The committee returned to Jesus with their half-used legal pads and a Xeroxed copy of the financial report. They determined that it would take a huge amount of money to feed such a crowd. They had it figured to the penny, and their figures were right. But their faith was wrong. Faith, you see, is always greater than the figures.

Meanwhile, one of the disciples decided not to give up. He decided to do what he could to alleviate the problem. Andrew, Simon's brother, canvassed the crowd for resources. He didn't come up with much, just one boy with five small barley loaves and two fish. (But it was more than the disciples had brought to the gathering.)

The dazed little boy was brought to the front of the crowd and presented to Jesus. By then, he was probably a little on the nervous side.

"Another of his disciples, Andrew, Simon Peter's brother, spoke up, 'Here is a boy with five small barley loaves and two small fish, but how far will they go among so many?'" (John 6:8-9).

With a faith not much stronger than a moustache on a mouse, Andrew brought the meager supplies to Jesus with one of the best straight lines in scripture: "How far will they go among so many?"

If he only knew.

Before we get too sanctimonious over Philip's problem or Andrew's question, we ought to remember how often we church folk complain to God about our paltry resources. If only we had more money, workers, building space, parking lots, land, or singers in the praise team that could sing on pitch. If only we had a better preacher, sound system, keyboard, or video projector.

Often, we concentrate on our *lack* of resources and wish we had better *luck*. But God wants to show us that our lack is only the beginning of His abundance. And luck doesn't have anything to do with a miracle. He wants to show us exactly *how far they will go among so many.*

I love the way Jesus put it in the Gospel of Luke: "Don't be afraid of missing out. You're my dearest friends! The Father wants to give you the very kingdom itself. Be generous. Give to the poor. Get yourselves a bank that can't go bankrupt, a bank in heaven far from bankrobbers, safe from embezzlers, a bank you can bank on. It's obvious, isn't it? The place where your treasure is, is the place you will most want to be, and end up being" (12:32-34, TM).

All the while we are concentrating on the problem, God is thinking about the solution.

THE SOLUTION IS IN JESUS' HANDS—NOT OURS

"Jesus said, 'Have the people sit down.' There was plenty of grass in that place, and the men sat down, about five thousand of them. Jesus then took the loaves, gave thanks, and distributed to those who were seated as much as they wanted. He did the same with the fish" (John 6:10-11).

Jesus had at least three options for solving this problem. He could tell the disciples to send the people away. No people, no problem. Or, He could solve the problem in the obvious way, by sending someone to the grocery store. Of course, that would have required a spur-of-the-moment fund drive to cover the cost of the grocery bill—the first capital campaign in Church history. Or, He could teach a world-class lesson in faith, and use the kid's lunch.

He used the kid's lunch.

Do you remember the disciple's question: *But how far will they go among so many?* Obviously, five barley loaves and two small fish weren't enough food to feed this crowd. Jesus didn't answer the question directly (and sometimes He doesn't answer our questions directly either). He simply instructed the disciples to have the people sit in groups of 50 or 100. The unparalleled miracle was about to be parceled out. And we know from experience that sometimes our miracles come in small groupings rather than in one lump sum.

But here's what you can learn from the situation: The first step toward a miracle is turning everything over to Jesus. Give everything you have left completely to Him, and let Him turn your *left-outs* into *leftovers*.

Make the move. It has miraculous potential.

One sports writer gave some good insight into the "paralysis of analysis." Baseball great Barry Bonds is a dangerous hitter anytime, and he is especially dangerous in the clutch. If you added a rookie pitcher to that equation, you got a situation that favored Bonds and the San Francisco Giants.

At least the rookie pitcher in this story seemed to think so. The Giants were behind by two runs, but they had just put two runners on base. Into the game came the rookie to face Bonds. Barry had gone hitless that day, but that hardly raised the kid's confidence. The catcher called for a slider. The kid shook it off. The catcher signaled a curve. Again the pitcher shook it off. After two more signs (fastball and change-up) had been rejected, the catcher called time and strolled to the mound.

"Look, kid," he said, "you've only got four pitches, and you've shaken them all off. What's your game plan?"

The kid glanced toward the plate at Barry Bonds and replied, "My plan is to hold on to this ball as long as I can."*

Unlike the pitcher in the story, inaction in the face of challenges can spell disaster for you. Just like the lad with the lunch, you must release it to Jesus.

Jesus took the boy's lunch, blessed it, and turned the meager supplies of the lunch bag into a banquet for the multitudes. The miracle was in His hands . . . not theirs.

Matthew's Gospel lets us in on some behind-the-scenes negotiations that led up to that miracle.

"That evening the disciples came to him and said, 'This is a desolate place, and it is getting late. Send the crowds away so they can go to the villages and buy food for themselves.'

"But Jesus replied, 'That isn't necessary—you feed them'" (Matt. 14:15-16, NLT).

We're not manufacturers. We're distributors. The sooner we get that principle straight in our lives, the sooner we move into miracle territory and the sooner the miracle of multiplication takes place. Everything we give to Jesus *multiplies* miraculously! He taught us that a tiny mustard seed grows into a mighty oak tree when we bury it in the soil of belief.

Watch this sequence. First, the loaves and fishes were in the little boy's mother's hands. Then they were in the boy's hands. Then they were in Andrew's hands. And finally they were in Jesus' hands. Not a single portion of food touched an outstretched hand that day that hadn't first been in the hands of Jesus. A total of perhaps 15,000 people were fed. It probably took all afternoon to distribute the food. And it all came from the hands of Jesus.

So when we hold up our sandwich toward heaven, when we give of our means for the Kingdom, we are giving to a God who can multiply our gifts just as He did on that hillside those many years ago. We are giving to a God who, in His own person, set the example for giving by sending His only Son as the Bread of Life from heaven.

"Begin to weave and God will provide the thread."
—German Proverb

GOD IS THE GOD OF "MATCHING GIFTS"

"When they had all had enough to eat, he said to his disciples, 'Gather the pieces that are left over. Let nothing be wasted.' So they gathered them and filled twelve baskets with the pieces of the five barley loaves left over by those who had eaten" (John 6:12-13).

There were enough leftovers to make the Saran Wrap people sing the "Hallelujah Chorus."

Friend, you may be a day late and a dollar short, but God isn't! He's always on time and He always has enough. No matter what you give to Him (whether it's in the form of dollars or a disaster), God takes it, blesses it, breaks it, and gives it back in a new, meaningful, and abundant form. And note that *there is always more given back than you can use*. God always gives in abundance.

From the time the lunch passed from the hands of the little boy through Andrew's hands to Jesus' hands and finally into the hands of the hungry crowd, it had multiplied—are you ready for this—at least *five thousand-fold*, perhaps as much as *fifteen thousand-fold*.

If you think about it, that scrawny little boy was carrying enough food to feed a small town! They didn't know it, and he didn't know it, but there it was, jostling around in his backpack just waiting for Jesus' hands. It was only about a pound of food. But God matched the little lunch with His great power, and the result was abundance. There is a principle here that every Christian needs to grab hold of. You never give anything to the cause of God that it doesn't multiply in some way before it reaches the point of need. Put it this way: *God is the God of matching gifts.* As the gospel songwriter so aptly put it:

Little is much when God is in it!
Labor not for wealth or fame.
There's a crown—and you can win it,
If you go in Jesus' name.

—Kittie L. Suffield

HOW WILL IT END?

On February 18, 2001, champion race car driver Dale Earnhardt took his final lap. The Daytona 500 stock car race looked like a hundred others, and so did the crash. But in an instant, Earnhardt was dead. NASCAR's greatest hero was gone. Millions of people around the world paused to pay tribute to this racing legend. At the age of 49, Dale Earnhardt had achieved what very few others have accomplished in *any* sport.

Soon it was said—and I think it's true—that Dale Earnhardt died while doing the thing that he loved most. That caused me to think about my own life. What do I want to be doing when my time comes? What about you? What do you want to be doing on the last day of your life? Playing golf? I doubt it. Traveling? Probably not. Sitting in a business meeting? No. What, then?

I'm sure that every one of us would like to reach the end of life doing the things that matter most.

And if that's true of our *last* breath, it's also true of our *latest* breath. Meaningful living comes from a surrender of ourselves (and our situations) to God. Only He can poke sunbeams through the dark clouds. Only He can build a temple out of the rubble. Only He can make a miracle out of a mess.

Your job is minuscule compared to His. You simply do what you can do, from the smallest faithful action to the simplest belief, and leave the rest to God. If He can number, name, and order the motion of 10 trillion planets, He can move your life through the maze of these times.

And these are times unlike any other. The tragic day of September 11, 2001, when America was attacked by terrorists moved the clock ahead even more, and we all stood helplessly by as the casualty count added up.

It's still being added. The effects are far-reaching—maybe reaching into your own heart. Even after the dust has settled you still may be wondering whether there is any rhyme or reason to your life. Someone said, "When we come to the end of ourselves, we have come to the beginning of God." His miracle power begins when we give Him the rudder of our ship. Two people can't steer without resulting in confusion and the potential for sending some undeserving dolphins to the judgment.

When you reach the end of trying to solve the problems, you have come to the place where God can move in. Sometimes all He needs is a tiny lunch in a shoulder bag to fill the emptiness of the multitudes.

---

*Emerson Falls, *The Executive Speechwriter Newsletter* (St. Johnsburg, Vt.), Vol. 15 No. 6.

When You Pray for Rain—
Wear a Raincoat
(You Gotta Believe It in Order to See It)

By faith, Noah built a ship in the middle of dry land. He was warned about something he couldn't see, and acted on what he was told. The result? His family was saved" (Heb. 11:7, TM).

Some people insist on being first in everything. Whether it's golf scores or gall bladder surgery, these folks insist on topping any story you tell. One such man prided himself on having all the latest gadgets for his car. One day while he sat idling at a stoplight, a young man pulled up alongside him in an old, beat-up Volkswagen and waved a sheet of fax paper, yelling, "Look what I've got! Need me to send a fax for you?" Not to be outdone, the gadget guru had a fax machine installed in his car that very afternoon.

A few days later, the fellow was out driving again and spotted the old Volkswagen. It was parked at the curb, and its windows were steamed up. The man immediately parked behind the VW and rapped on the windshield. When the young man appeared the proud fellow waved a newly received fax at him and said, "Look! I've got a fax machine too." The young fellow gave him a scornful look and said with disgust, "You got me out of the shower just to tell me that?"

But there are some stories you just can't top. That's what the fellow discovered who had survived a West Virginia flood. That flood was the most memorable experience of his life, and he never stopped talking about it. When he died and went to heaven, he asked Peter if he could have a few minutes during the midweek service to tell the people about his experiences.

"Sure," said Peter. "We can arrange that. But you might want to know that Noah's leading the service."

That's a fable. But here's a true one that just can't be topped. You know the story of Noah—the crazy guy who built a boat on dry land. What made him do it? When you think about it, it wasn't a very logical thing to do—building an ark while the sun was still shining and without a raindrop in sight. Probably the neighbors were wondering if ol' Noah had "both oars in the water," so to speak. Every day as they did their morning power walk past Noah's place, his nosy neighbors wondered about the strange building project.

Now, before we get so high and mighty (or maybe I should say, "high and dry"), we'll have to admit that we probably would have had a few questions of our own. So why did he do it?

You might say, "Lots of folk build boats on dry land." (You've heard of dry dock, right?) You've got me there. But, here's the difference between "lots of folk" and Noah. Most people build a boat on dry land expecting to take it to the water. Noah built a boat on dry land, *expecting the water to come to it.*

Noah had no proof that it would rain. He didn't have a computer-calculated weather forecast. He didn't even get the Weather Channel on his satellite dish.

He wasn't a meteorologist. Up till then, the only way he knew there was going to be any precipitation was by that aching in his knee, the result of a torn ligament during the Mesopotamia all-star softball tournament.

There was no visible indication of any impending natural disaster. The only thing Noah had to go on was God's word. God told him to do it, *and that was all Noah needed*. He had a believe-it kind of faith.

Faith means taking God at His word. It means believing things you can't even see simply because God said they were out there. Faith makes it possible to accept what we cannot prove. Faith is the force that makes mountains move, blind eyes see, and dead souls leap back to life. And it all starts on dry land. It all happens the moment you say, "I believe it."

Top 10 Lessons from Noah's Ark

10. We're all in the same boat.
9. Plan ahead. It wasn't raining when Noah started building the ark.
8. Stay fit. God might ask you to do something big when you're 600.
7. Always travel in pairs.
6. When feeling overwhelmed, remember, the ark was built by amateurs, the *Titanic* was built by professionals.
5. Look for the rainbow at the end of the storms of life.
4. Don't name your son after pig parts.
3. Be sure to follow God's blueprint.

31

2. Find grace in the eyes of the Lord.

1. Don't miss the boat.

Believe-it faith begins with listening to God's Word. "By his faith he condemned the world" (Heb. 11:7).

God's commentary was more important to Noah than the world's questionings. But first he had to learn how to listen.

Let me illustrate. Translating God's Word into a tribal language is a challenging task. One missionary was troubled by his inability to effectively communicate the idea of obedience. This was a concept that the natives seldom practiced or valued. His translation block was broken one day when he whistled for his dog and the animal came running at full speed. An old native was impressed by the dog's responsiveness and admiringly said in the native tongue, "Your dog is all ear." The missionary had his word for obedience, and it's a pretty good translation for us. We could even translate the prophet Samuel's advice: "To be all ear is better than sacrifice" (1 Sam. 15:22).[1]

That's what Peter found out when he met Jesus. Luke tells the story of a miracle that began with obedience. Luke 5:1-7:

> One day as Jesus was standing by the Lake of Gennesaret, with the people crowding around him and listening to the word of God, he saw at the water's edge two boats, left there by the fishermen, who were washing their nets. He got into one of the boats, the one belonging to Simon, and asked him to put out a little from shore. Then he sat down and taught the people from the boat.
>
> When he had finished speaking, he said to Simon, "Put out into deep water, and let down the nets for a catch."
>
> Simon answered, "Master, we've worked hard all night and haven't caught anything. But because you say so, I will let down the nets."

When they had done so, they caught such a large number of fish that their nets began to break. So they signaled their partners in the other boat to come and help them, and they came and filled both boats so full that they began to sink.

The writer of Hebrews makes the same point about our need to believe what God says. "The fundamental fact of existence is that this trust in God, this faith, is the firm foundation under everything that makes life worth living. It's our handle on what we can't see" (11:1, TM). Faith is not about talk; it's about trust.

The Bible is full of examples of faith. Faith turned Moses, a stammering herdsman, into the leader of a nation—the deliverer of God's people. Faith caused Abraham, an elderly man, to start on a journey even though he didn't know where he would wind up. He simply believed the promise of God. (And by the way, believing God's word also resulted in fatherhood for Abraham, 20 or so years past his first Social Security check.) Faith gave three timid teens—Shadrach, Meshach, and Abednego—enough boldness to stand up to a king and refuse to bow to idols. Faith made the walls of Jericho crumble like an imploded old baseball stadium.

And faith still works. After all these years, God's people still take up their pails and shovels and move mountains. God's people still drop dollars into offering plates and see church buildings grow out of them. From the journals of 10 million saints the message echoes across time: "I believed it . . . and then I saw it with my own eyes . . ."

Faith is the slab on which God builds His kingdom. The great evangelist D. L. Moody said, "Behind every work of God you will always find some kneeling soul." It's strange but true, God's people see better on their knees than the world does on its tiptoes. In prayerful listening to the promises of God, common folks like you and me are motivated to move out and claim enemy territories.

We're motivated to set sail even when we're standing on dry land.

Believe-it faith is willing to act with courage when everyone else is fearful.

"By his faith he condemned the world" (Heb. 11:7). Noah's beliefs were in stark contrast to those around him. The people of Noah's day needed a money-back guarantee, signed, sealed, and notarized at the county courthouse. Noah simply needed a word from God. That made the world's faith look smaller than the dot in a web site address.

I've always admired the swimmer in the group who's willing to go first into the water. It may be 60 degrees Fahrenheit, and the water may be 5 degrees cooler than that, but there's usually some guy in the crowd who's willing to take the first plunge. I've also admired his bold claims—sometimes to my own discomfort—to "Come on in, the water's fine." He stands up, knee-high in ice water, with a frozen smile on his face, confidence in the voice, and enough goose bumps on his forearms to form a landing strip for the Goodyear blimp. But I believed him.

Faith is willing to be the first (or, as in my case, even the second) to jump in. It's willing to risk everything with one daring dive. And most often, being "that far from the sandbar" is the safest place to be. It's like the classic story of the novice golfer who cringed as he spent 15 minutes looking for a sliced drive off the tee only to discover the lost golf ball had landed on top of an anthill. Choosing a sand wedge, he positioned himself and slashed at the half-buried ball three times. By the fourth stroke, sand and ants were flying everywhere. Everything was in motion except the golf ball. Again the duffer braced and swung. Again the anthill was devastated, but the ball lay unmoved. Soon a panic-stricken voice boomed over the intercom in the anthill. "ATTENTION ALL ANTS. ATTENTION ALL ANTS. MOVE TO THE GOLF BALL IMMEDIATELY. MOVE TO THE GOLF BALL IMMEDIATELY. YOU'LL BE SAFE IF YOU GET ON THE BALL."

It's a lesson fit for humans as well as ants: If you're going to survive—if you're going to put the promises of God to a well-proven test—you'll have to get on the ball. Faith requires positive action.

It's important to notice several other things about Noah's faith.

First, he built the ark without ever seeing rain. He didn't need to "see it" in order to believe it. Our faith isn't built just on the things we can see. Moses, another member of Faith's Hall of Fame, had that same kind of belief. Heb. 11:27 tells us, "It was by faith that Moses left Egypt and was not afraid of the king's anger. Moses continued strong as if he could see the God that no one can see" (NCV).

In fact, most of our faith-facts aren't even in the line of sight. That even includes our faith in Christ. 1 Pet. 1:8 says, "Though you have not seen him, you love him; and even though you do not see him now, you believe in him and are filled with an inexpressible and glorious joy." We don't need a "Jesus sighting" in order to believe in Him. We walk and talk with Him by faith. By faith, we see His lonely walk to Calvary and claim its merits. By faith, we call His name in times of trouble and believe with all of our hearts that He's listening.

When my sons, Seth and Adam, were small they would sometimes get into troubling situations. Whether it was a broken training wheel on a bicycle or the threatened punch in the nose by the neighborhood bully, they knew that a call to Dad would bring some action.

"DAD."

They didn't even have to see me to know that help was nearby. They believed in me. They staked their confidence on my presence—even when they couldn't see me.

Second, Noah's family members were the only God-fearing believers in the community. He was willing to stand with those who stood for God—no matter how few they were in number. Faith doesn't need a club. It doesn't stand on hand-holding. It stands wholly on the written and whispered promises of a God who cannot lie and will not fail.

Noah's experience illustrates the frequently forgotten truth that the crowd is often wrong. Noah stood against public opinion for 120 years because he believed God. Rebecca Olsen put it this way, "Noah realized he was the one to influence the crowd, rather than the one who was influenced by it. He established a priority and then for one hundred and twenty years, day after day, his hands built the Ark while his mouth proclaimed salvation."[2]

To stand *against* a crowd and to stand *for* Jesus requires a firm conviction of the truth of God's Word *and* the courage to act upon it. Faith doesn't wait for green lights. It moves forward and waits for a red light. James makes the relationship between faith and action crystal clear: "Faith by itself, if it is not accompanied by action, is dead. But someone will say, 'You have faith; I have deeds.' Show me your faith without deeds, and I will show you my faith by what I do" (James 2:17-18).

Believe-it faith is willing to obey God regardless of the outcome.

What is the opposite of faith? Unbelief. Unbelief causes us to see only the problem—which in turn obscures our vision of God.

"Unbelief puts your problem between you and God;
Believe-it faith puts God between you and your problem."

It's easy to talk believe-it faith, it's even easy to have believe-it faith for others. Like the two little brothers who walked into the dentist's office. The older brother said, "Look, Doc, we've got a bad tooth, and we're kinda in a hurry. Could ya just skip the Novocain and yank it out?"

The dentist replied, "My, what a brave young man. Let's have a look at that tooth."

The older brother says to his little brother, "Show 'im your tooth, Tommy."

What was the result of Noah's belief? The Bible says he "became one of those who are made right with God through faith" (Heb. 11:7, CEV). Faith was just the beginning. Noah moved to the next level. He was marked as a believer. He became *Exhibit A* that God keeps His word.

Legend has it that Noah's youngest son came to him and asked if he could fish off the bow of the ark once it got in the water.

And Noah supposedly replied, "I don't know for sure, Son. But if you do, you're going to have to go easy on the bait. You'll only have two worms."

Almost everything about Noah's future cruise was unknown to him—including a safe landing. When God told him he was to take two of every kind of animal into the ark, he wasn't even sure how he would get all those cages cleaned before the floodwaters subsided.

But he was willing to trust God, even if all the facts weren't in the file folder of his heart. God hadn't missed a payment on any previous promise. That's why Noah loved Him so. And that's why God's heart was touched by Noah's faith. You see, for every step that you take toward God, He'll take two steps toward you.

Noah didn't have any way of knowing what the outcome of his voyage would be. But by faith, he obeyed God, and God secured the results.

He obediently prepared the ark for the salvation of his family. And that's another important principle of Noah's faith: Faith casts a ray of light. When someone is willing to walk in the light of God's promises, it will always help someone else find his or her way.

Noah and his family were saved because they believed God's rain forecast, even when the nightly news called for partly sunny days.

And did it ever rain.

Sooner than you'd ever think, nothing was the same in Noah's community. Water wings and inflatable rafts were flying off the shelves at the local Wal-Mart. And those who laughed at Noah's message were rolling and packing their panicky questions into bottles, hoping they would eventually float his way. Maybe someday one of the bottles would wash to shore and they would be able to find out where they went wrong.

Noah and his passengers weren't on the proverbial "three-hour-tour" of TV land. This wasn't a *Gilligan's Island* journey. This was the real thing. Reality TV had turned to reality living. But Noah's crew had obediently followed God's detailed instructions. The outcome? The crew survived. And, the captain was inducted into the Hall of Fame. Heb. 11:13-16:

All these people were still living by faith when they died. They did not receive the things promised; they only saw them and welcomed them from a distance. And they admitted that they were aliens and strangers on earth. People who say such things show that they are looking for a country of their own. If they had been thinking of the country they had left, they would have had opportunity to return. Instead, they were longing for a better country—a heavenly one. Therefore God is not ashamed to be called their God, for he has prepared a city for them.

Forget about having a fund-raiser for that Hall of Fame. You couldn't raise enough to pay for its splendor. It's out of this world.

I don't know if there are pictures on the wall or sculptured figures in the hallway. I do know that all the exhibits are live exhibits. I do know that the caretaker is the same as the Creator. And I also know that each of the honorees would say it was worth every effort that led to their induction.

My longtime friend Congressman Bob McEwen took his young son to a McDonald's restaurant and purchased a large order of french fries for him. You know how good McDonald's fries smell! (That's all I'm allowed to do, smell them!) As he sat watching his son eat them, Bob reached out instinctively and grabbed one. The little fellow playfully slapped his father's hand and said, "Dad, you can't have one. Those aren't your fries!"

Bob said three thoughts immediately went through his mind: First, he thought, *I'm the one who brought him here and bought the fries with my own money. Without me, he would have no fries.* The next thought, *My son has forgotten who's in control of the fries. I could take them away from him instantly, or I could buy him a truckload of those fries. I am the source of the fries.* Finally Bob realized, *I could go get my own fries if I wanted to.* The congressman concluded, *What I really want is for my son to be unselfish.*

God wants us to learn a similar lesson. The stars will still shine brilliantly. Soft rains will still moisten blades of spring grass. The seven oceans will still play tag with their shorelines. Nothing will change if we don't live by faith—except us. We thrive only as we depend upon Him. He is our Source. When we let go of our lives and give them to Him, when we start building ships in the desert, we will begin to reap the benefits of *believe-it* faith. Then, "Man the lifeboats."

When you start taking God at His word even in the worst of times, the best is yet to come. "Without faith it is impossible to please God, because anyone who comes to him must believe that he exists and that he rewards those who earnestly seek him" (Heb. 11:6). Did you catch that? He rewards those who earnestly seek Him.

I like the classic story of the little girl standing with her farmer dad at a prayer meeting. The community was experiencing one of its worst droughts ever. The farmers were so concerned they gathered out in one of the fields and began to beg God for some rain.

The curious daughter looked at the crowd and motioned for her father to lean over so she could whisper a message. "What?" the dad replied, a little annoyed that she would interrupt this great showing of faith.

"Dad," she said softly, "does everyone here believe that God can send us some rain?"

"Of course they do," the father said curtly, as he straightened back up.

Soon there was another tug at his sleeve, and another motioning for him to bend down to hear another whisper.

"What is it now?" the tall father replied as he leaned over and cupped his ear to hear the next question.

"Dad, if they all believe that God is going to send the rain, how come we're the only ones wearin' raincoats?"

Here is James the apostle's nomination of another inductee in Faith's Hall of Fame: "The prayer of a righteous man is powerful and effective. Elijah was a man just like us. He prayed earnestly that it would not rain, and it did not rain on the land for three and a half years. Again he prayed, and the heavens gave rain, and the earth produced its crops" (James 5:16-18).

He had enough trust in the divine to believe that He would even alter the course of nature to show His Lordship over life.

Believe-it faith prepares for the storm by preparing the heart, first. In fact, *believe-it* faith can be working on heart conditioning even in the midst of a storm. Whether you have a boatload of zoo citizens or whether you're sailing solo, you can raise the sails of hope. God can be trusted in the trying times of your life—and He'll never be a moment late with a miracle.

---

1. *Moody,* July/August 1997, 36.

2. Rebecca Olsen, "Building for Life," *Decision,* November 1987, 33-35.

When You Have a Wedding
It's a Good Idea to Invite Jesus
(Inviting Christ into Your Life)

One of the earliest TV talk shows involved a kindly and fatherly host interviewing a panel of early elementary schoolchildren. The host, TV pioneer Art Linkletter, managed to pry some of TV's funniest comments out of the children, who were often mugging for their parents in the audience as much as to the cameras. The naive candor of their responses provoked howls of laughter from the audience and prompted the famous Linkletter line that resulted in his best-selling book, *Kids Say the Darndest Things.*

On one program, Linkletter asked a little girl, "What's your favorite Bible story?"

"When He turned the water into wine," she responded, partially revealing the story of the well-known New Testament event.

Linkletter knew the rest of the story and filled in most of

the details in his own mind. Knowing that he had one of those precious moments in the making, he asked, "And what's the moral of that story?"

She replied with more than a cute ad-lib. She uttered one of those "a little child shall lead them" bits of wisdom: "When you have a wedding, it's a good idea to have Jesus there."

We already know what happens when Jesus goes to a wedding. A party is bound to break out. Here is the story of one such occurrence from John's Gospel.

> On the third day a wedding took place at Cana in Galilee. Jesus' mother was there, and Jesus and his disciples had also been invited to the wedding. When the wine was gone, Jesus' mother said to him, "They have no more wine."
>
> "Dear woman, why do you involve me?" Jesus replied. "My time has not yet come."
>
> His mother said to the servants, "Do whatever he tells you."

Mary was smart. She knew the only way to resolve lack in our lives—whether it be wine, health, love—is to do whatever He tells us to do.

> Nearby stood six stone water jars, the kind used by the Jews for ceremonial washing, each holding from twenty to thirty gallons.
>
> Jesus said to the servants, "Fill the jars with water"; so they filled them to the brim.

These servants were smart. They not only obeyed Jesus but gave it their all as well. They displayed brimful obedience.

> Then he told them, "Now draw some out and take it to the master of the banquet."

They did so, and the master of the banquet tasted the water that had been turned into wine. He did not realize where it had come from, though the servants who had drawn the water knew. Then he called the bridegroom aside and said, "Everyone brings out the choice wine first and then the cheaper wine after the guests have had too much to drink; but you have saved the best till now."

This, the first of his miraculous signs, Jesus performed at Cana in Galilee. He thus revealed his glory, and his disciples put their faith in him *(John 2:1-11)*.

But it goes further than a wedding day. "It's a good idea to have Jesus there" on every occasion. You may not be planning a wedding. Sadly, you may be planning a memorial service for a friend or loved one.

Your occasion may not even include a formal ceremony. You may simply be planning a day in court. Maybe you have that appointment with the doctor.

Or your once-bright and beautiful relationship may suddenly be coming to a painful ending.

Or you may be entering a new relationship.

Whatever the occasion, it's always a good idea to invite Jesus to be there.

That's clearly seen in the attitudes and actions that surrounded the wedding recorded in the Bible.

In a matter-of-fact way, the apostle and New Testament writer John tells us about the time that Jesus and His disciples were invited to a wedding. "On the third day a wedding took place at Cana in Galilee. Jesus' mother was there, and Jesus and his disciples had also been invited to the wedding" (John 2:1).

There's no use trying to lift Jesus from real life. He was—and still is—always right in the middle of it. Fully God, and yet fully man, the God-man, Jesus Christ, understands our life because He experienced our living. He was just as familiar with dusty roads as He was with golden thrones. He left the majesty of heaven for a firsthand experience with the mess of earth.

How else could He be such an understanding friend? How else could He have offered himself as the sacrifice for our sin? He had to be one of us. He had to go to our weddings, our funerals, our courts, our sickrooms, and our dinners. So, it's not so surprising that He went to this wedding.

Since many of the disciples were from Cana, they probably knew the bride and groom very well. It was a great day of friendship. But it was a memorable day for more reasons than the candlelighting, soprano solo, appetizers, or those little paper cups of pastel-colored mints and peanuts. It was on this wedding day that Jesus performed the first miracle recorded in the Scriptures.

Of all Jesus' miracles, I believe this one is the most significant. Why? First, because marriage—at its best—is one of the highest expressions of human love and commitment. God created and ordained the home by the earliest lights of the first dawn. Jesus reflected on that importance of setting up a home when the religious zealots of His day asked Him some questions about marriage and divorce. "Don't you know that in the beginning the Creator made a man and a woman? That's why a man leaves his father and mother and gets married. He becomes like one person with his wife. Then they are no longer two people, but one. And no one should separate a couple that God has joined together" (Matt. 19:4-6, CEV).

Second, I believe it is significant because it represents more than a wedding—it represents life, with its joys, its beginnings, its endings, and its continuing challenges. Here, we can learn as much about living as we can about marrying.

And granted, some "marrying" occasions are learning experiences.

As a pastor, I've always enjoyed performing weddings. Not just because they are such a solemn and meaningful celebration, but also because you never know what's going to happen next.

Ring bearers throw up.

Flower girls fall down.

Veils catch fire.

Grown men faint.

Vows are forgotten.

The "best man" loses the ring. (Which makes you wonder what's so great about him if he can't even remember to bring one ring to the wedding.) And talking about rings, I love the story of the little boy who was in a relative's wedding. As he was coming down the aisle, he would take two steps, stop, turn to the crowd, put up his hands like claws, and roar. So it went, step, step, ROAR, step, step, ROAR all the way down the aisle. The congregation couldn't help but laugh.

The little boy, however, became more and more distressed. When he reached the minister, he asked why the congregation was laughing so hard. "After all," the little boy explained, "I was being the ring bear."

And sometimes, the participants even fail to show up (including either one of the "Wilt Thou" folk).

In at least six ways, weddings represent all of life.

1. Anything can happen—*and usually does.*

2. They are supposed to be joyous. (Though sometimes you have to look for the light. Attending a wedding for the first

time, a little girl whispered to her mother, "Why is the bride wearing white?" Her mother said, "Because white is the color of happiness, and today is the happiest day of her life." The little girl thought about this for a minute, then asked, "Then why is the groom wearing black?")

3. They include both laughter and tears. (And nobody lives very long without either.)

4. Everyone is supposed to get along.

5. Sooner or later, mother will get a new dress.

6. Dad usually gets stuck with the bill.

Weddings, then, not only mark the *beginning* of a wonderful, happy life but also *reflect* this life.

As another example, one wedding went off without a hitch until the preacher concluded the ceremony by saying, "I now pronounce you husband and wife"—forgetting the much-anticipated benedictory smooch. As flustered as he was, the bridegroom hadn't forgotten it, however. In fact, he had been looking forward to it. Still a little nervous, he got his words a bit turned around when he asked the forgetful preacher out loud, "Isn't it *kisstomary* to *cuss* the bride?"

The preacher smiled and said, "No, son. Not until you've been married a little while longer."

If the presence of Jesus is important at a wedding, then it's important during the rest of life as well. It really is a good idea to invite Jesus.

Top Ten Signs It's Going to Be a Tough Wedding

10. The groom says, "Premarital counseling? I don't need that, I've been married three times."

9. The ushers ask guests, "Smoking or nonsmoking?"

8. The groomsmen are wearing orange hunting vests.
7. There's a two-dollar cover charge at the door.
6. The bride has three stepfathers who all insist on ushering her down the aisle.
5. The mother of the bride impatiently yells, "Hurry it up, preacher, you're gonna make me late for bingo."
4. The processional song is "Brick House" by the Commodores.
3. The ceremony is conducted by the local square-dance caller.
2. The best man is wearing handcuffs and is escorted by a corrections officer.
1. The unity candle goes out.

THE PRESENCE OF JESUS TURNS A WEDDING DAY INTO A BLESSED DAY

"Jesus and his disciples had also been invited to the wedding."

This young couple was evidently well known to Mary and Jesus. The Lord may have sold wood products to people in Cana. He was a carpenter, after all, and Cana was near Nazareth. Mary evidently felt responsible to see that things went well at the wedding banquet, so there may have been some family connection. At any rate, the young couple didn't hesitate to invite them to their wedding.

By the way, no one should feel hesitant about inviting Jesus to his or her wedding.

This true story exemplifies just that. A young man, let's call him Jeff, began thinking of marriage. He was a little anxious about the whole thing, but he knew what he wanted in a marriage partner, so he started an earnest search. He went out of his way to meet several girls. He was attracted to some, but only one stole his heart—let's call her Anna. He began to develop a relationship with Anna, and to his great joy, she returned his affection. They fell in love, and one evening—after the third re-fill of 7-Up at Steak & Shake—he finally got up enough nerve to propose marriage.

Their families were thrilled at the news, and word of the en-gagement also quickly spread among their friends. Jeff and An-na couldn't hide their joy as they started planning their wed-ding. They chose the date. They contacted the minister. They talked about the flowers and candles and the ceremony and the food. Then came the guest list: who to invite? They started compiling names. They would invite their parents, grandpar-ents, relatives, of course. Their friends and their work associates.

And then Jeff came up with an interesting idea, or perhaps it was Anna.

"What would you think of inviting Jesus himself? Let's add Him to the wedding list just as we'd invite anyone else. Let's send Him a formal invitation to join the celebration of our marriage."

So they did—and by His Spirit, Jesus Christ came to their wedding. (When He is invited to any occasion, He always glad-ly accepts!)

As a matter of fact, Jesus always *wants* to attend our wed-dings. All you need for a marriage is a license, a witness, and a preacher—except maybe a bride and a groom. But a *good mar-riage* requires the presence of Christ.

Oh, how He wants to be there. He wants to help build a marriage out of a ceremony. He wants to live in our homes and bring purpose and peace. He wants to help two people merge their uniqueness into a oneness. Robert Morgan said, "A Chris-tian marriage has the presence of Jesus Christ in it, filling the house, casting his glow on the home, and making the relation-ships spiritual and special. And that makes all the difference."

But He also wants to be present at our other occasions as well. He wants to bring His courage to our daily duties. He wants to help us blend with others. He wants to fill our lives and our living with so much joy that it will get all over anyone who is near.

His presence turns a regular day into a blessed day.

The Presence of Jesus Turns a Need into a Supply

Miracles happen when we understand that Jesus cares about our everyday needs, not just our spiritual needs. He cares about people being unnecessarily embarrassed. He cares about people enjoying themselves. Jesus is the kind of person you want at your party. He knows how to have a good time.

The wedding celebration was going along as expected, when suddenly a problem arose. (And isn't that just like life?) The wine was gone. The "punch" of Jesus' day was suddenly missing from the borrowed, crystal-looking, plastic punch bowl.

"Jesus' mother said to him, 'They have no more wine.'" (Such a typical mom, pointing out the obvious.)

Jesus responded tenderly and yet firmly, knowing that His entire life was on a divinely appointed schedule. "'Dear woman, why do you involve me?' Jesus replied. 'My time has not yet come.'"

Then in an awesome moment of devotion to her son, Mary acknowledges His Lordship. "His mother said to the servants, 'Do whatever he tells you.'"

Need would soon turn to supply.

"Nearby stood six stone water jars, the kind used by the Jews for ceremonial washing, each holding from twenty to thirty gallons. Jesus said to the servants, 'Fill the jars with water;' so they filled them to the brim."

Here's a good lesson: If we would simply invite Him to the occasions of our life, Jesus can use the simplest, least obvious resources to turn our want into His plenty.

Here's another lesson, using the theory of "supply and demand": Christ's supply often follows His demand.

"Then he told them, 'Now draw some out and take it to the master of the banquet.'

"They did so, and the master of the banquet tasted the water that had been turned into wine. He did not realize where it had come from."

Their obedience to Jesus resulted in a miracle. It always does.

Jesus said, "I tell you the truth, anyone who has faith in me will do what I have been doing. He will do even greater things than these, because I am going to the Father. And I will do whatever you ask in my name, so that the Son may bring glory to the Father. You may ask me for anything in my name, and I will do it.

"If you love me, you will obey what I command" *(John 14:12-15)*.

He wants to turn need into supply—our water into wine. He wants to transform the ordinary of our lives into something special.

Having been told to fill the pots with water, the servants filled them to the brim in complete obedience. Then the miracle happened. As the water was poured out, it could be seen that it had turned to wine.

What Jesus did was to speed up the process of nature. It took Creator Jesus only an instant, not a season, to produce the wine.

God is always on time to our occasions because He is the Lord of time—time bows to His wishes.

The presence of the Lord Jesus turned the threatening sorrow of that wedding scene into a celebration that has been an example of joy throughout history. And He can turn the aching wants of your life into abundant supply as well.

THE PRESENCE OF JESUS TURNS FEAR AND FAILURE INTO FAITH

The banquet master's job was on the line. The wine was gone—and he was in charge of its supply to the wedding guests. But Jesus taught more than one lesson that day. Not only did He use the occasion to give a PowerPoint presentation on His Lordship, but He also taught about His love. And the banquet master passed the course with an A. "Then he called the bridegroom aside and said, 'Everyone brings out the choice wine first and then the cheaper wine after the guests have had too much to drink; but you have saved the best till now.'" He learned that Jesus was not just about *quantity* but also about *quality*. John 10:10, "I have come that they may have life, and have it to the full."

True living isn't about how much stuff we can squeeze into our lives. It's about quality. You can have a lot of the world's stuff and be utterly miserable. Conversely, you can have little of the world's stuff and be deliriously happy. The difference: Jesus.

What are you afraid of? Poverty? Insignificance? Rejection?

Jesus can turn that water into wine. He can even make faith out of fear.

What miracle is needed in your marriage right now? Invite Jesus to come over. What miracles do you need in the rest of your life? Use that same guest list.

Jesus turned human failure into a heavenly success. Erwin Lutzer said, "We forget that God is a specialist; He is well able to work our failures into His plans."

We always put the best foot forward and then mourn when the refreshments are gone. But when Jesus Christ comes into a life, He starts with the best and then the best continues to get better. The apostle Paul tried to express it, "God can do anything, you know—far more than you could ever imagine or guess or request in your wildest dreams!" (Eph. 3:20, TM).

THE PRESENCE OF JESUS INSPIRES A LIFELONG COMMITMENT

"He thus revealed his glory, and his disciples put their faith in him."

Seeing Jesus perform this miracle had a dramatic effect on the disciples. They were ready to follow Him anywhere—and they did.

Not everyone accepted Jesus for who He was. But those who did were changed by the experience. John 1:12, "To all who received him, to those who believed in his name, he gave the right to become children of God."

Study the life of Christ and the development of His relationship with the disciples between the wedding of Cana of Galilee and the Day of Pentecost. You'll see quite a change.

They developed a commitment to fellowship with one another. Jesus said, "You are my friends when you do the things I command you" (John 15:14, TM). And they did. They prayed together, talked together, traveled together, and worked together.

Everything changed when they met Jesus. When they invited Him into their lives, their lives took on a new meaning. Just like that wedding day in Cana, the presence of Jesus made the difference.

Don't you think it's a good idea to invite Jesus to all of our events? Shouldn't we invite Him to weddings, funerals, graduations, picnics, and into every aspect of our lives?

No One Is Immune to Problems—
Even the Lion Has to Fight Off Flies
(Seeing the Solution in the Situation)

On a recent trip to South Africa, I observed a stately lion resting in the afternoon sun. It was an impressive lion—regal, powerful, elegant, he truly was the epitome of the king of beasts. No animal—and few men—would challenge the authority of this awesome creature.

Resting contentedly on a hot day, he looked like he didn't have a care in the world except for those pesky flies. That lion's long tail was in constant motion, wagging back and forth, back and forth, back and forth . . . trying to keep a nagging swarm of flies at bay.

I thought to myself, "Even the king of the jungle has to fight flies." No life is free from annoyances.

> The LORD said to Moses, "Send some men to explore the land of Canaan, which I am giving to the Israelites. From each ancestral tribe send one of its leaders."

So at the LORD's command Moses sent them out from the Desert of Paran. All of them were leaders of the Israelites. . . .

They gave Moses this account: "We went into the land to which you sent us, and it does flow with milk and honey! Here is its fruit. But the people who live there are powerful, and the cities are fortified and very large. We even saw descendants of Anak there" *(Num. 13:1-2, 27-28).*

Talk about a *National Geographic* magazine article.

Jehovah God had promised His people, the Israelites, a new homeland. But it wasn't just any piece of real estate. This was real estate that would make Donald Trump salivate. This real estate was the land of promise.

Fascinating.

Unexplored.

Israel had been on the move ever since the Pharaoh of Egypt had ordered them to pack their Samsonites and get out of town. You remember the story. Forty years of wandering—with all the RVs and Sears' tents being set up and torn down for the next leg of the journey—had made them a bit journey-weary.

Then, the Lord put a global positioning system in Moses' heart and pointed him toward the final destination: Canaan, a land that had been prepared especially for them. But here's the kicker: it was a land meant for all of us as well. Canaan was a type of heaven—the final destination of every child of God.

(And who could disagree that our journey toward the "promised land" is sometimes just as tiring.)

So what does this place look like? Well, we only have a partial home tour of the final Canaan (heaven) given in the Scriptures. But the Promised Land of Moses' day was real-time real estate. It could be navigated. Surveyors could set their bright orange cones along its roads and hold up traffic while they measured the territory.

They did. And then they came back with their *National Geographic* article (and soon-to-be-released video).

"Well?" Moses asked. "Tell us about this Promised Land."

One of the leaders stumbled over his words a little as he drew nervous little lines in the sand with the toe sticking out of his sandals. "Uh . . . Well . . . We . . . Uh . . ."

"C'mon," Moses demanded.

"Well . . . Uh . . . Let's just put it this way: We've got some good news and some bad news."

"The good news?" Moses asked.

"Sure enough, it's everything God said it would be. It's a beautiful and fertile land. There are fruit and vegetable stands on every corner. Grapes the size of Volkswagens. Why, we even saw a couple of Starbucks coffee shops. It is *some* country," the advance team reported.

"And the bad news?" Moses pried.

"Uh . . . Well . . . Uh . . . We also saw some giants."

"Giants?"

"Yes, Moses. There were some soldiers in that land that made the center on a National Basketball Association team look smaller than a Kentucky Derby jockey. Moses, in comparison to them, we looked like grasshoppers."

Another member of the Advance Team, Caleb, spoke up disgustedly, "Oh, brother. Granted, there were some pretty tall soldiers guarding that land. But I know we can take 'em. After all, we have the Lord on our side."

The story (enhanced just a little) is so typical. Different folks looking at the same thing see things in their own way. Some look and see a problem. Others look at the same thing and see a solution.

I guess it's a lot like life—there are problems and solutions in just about everything.

Looking at life is a lot like looking at the Promised Land through the eyes of those visitors: There are some grapes. There are some giants. And sometimes we feel like grasshoppers.

We'd like to think that life could be full of blessings only. That would be great. But it's not realistic. In fact, life has its share of joys and sorrows, struggles and triumphs. And they're usually mixed together. Like one of those twist ice-cream cones, our lives are a combination of shadows and brightness.

There *are* some giants in our lives—*big* enough to make us feel as *small* as grasshoppers:

Bitterness.

Doubt.

Discouragement.

Infirmity.

Jealousy.

Disobedience.

Fear.

But the *grapes* of grace are greater than the *giants* of opposition.

Let's push the rewind button on that *National Geographic* video (now released) and take another look at some of those grapes. I think that in the process we'll learn a little about God's perfect power and God's perfect timing.

The Grapes of Abundance

"When they reached the Valley of Eshcol, they cut off a branch bearing a single cluster of grapes. Two of them carried it on a pole between them, along with some pomegranates and figs" (Num. 13:23).

Now, I'm not much of a horticulturist, but when I read about a cluster of grapes so big that it took two men to carry it, I'd say there was some abundance in Canaan.

No matter how barren the desert is in your life, if you'll look with enough patience and intensity, you're going to see some abundance. Even if the "giants" are guarding the cafeteria line, God will have a *2-for-one* coupon to the local fast-food stashed somewhere. Let's face it, He has pledged himself to take care of you. "My God will use his wonderful riches in Christ Jesus to give you everything you need" (Phil. 4:19, NCV).

The doubting members of Israel's Advance Team couldn't see the grapes for the giants. They didn't look far enough—or at least they didn't look at the right thing. If they had rubbed the sleepy giants from their eyes they would have seen some grapes—huge grapes, grapes of God's supply. And what's more, they would have seen that God had thrown in some pomegranates and figs for dessert.

Grapes? Abundance in enemy territory? You better *believe it.* God doesn't need friendly territory to set up a supply tent. Listen to the psalmist David as he sings a song of thanksgiving to his Lord, "Even though I walk through the valley of the shadow of death, I will fear no evil, for you are with me; your rod and your staff, they comfort me. You prepare a table before me in the presence of my enemies. You anoint my head with oil; my cup overflows" (Ps. 23:4-5).

Did you see it? "My cup overflows." Where? "In the presence of my enemies."

THE GRAPES OF AFFIRMATION

That South African king of the jungle had the annoyance of a swarm of flies. The members of Israel's Advance Team had a few annoyances too—but they also had the affirmation of the team.

Two of them carried it [the grape clusters] on a pole between them.

Now, I'm sure that if he had given it the "ol' college try" one of those fellas could have mustered enough strength to drag those grapes back to the pickup truck by himself.

But God likes teamwork.

Jesus could have spread the gospel news across the land all by himself, for example. But instead He chose, trained, nurtured, and deployed a company of disciples. He duplicated His efforts in the lives of others during that intense three-year period prior to His crucifixion.

Jesus and the disciples affirmed each other—even when the political and religious zealots were drumming up the opposition against them. (When they were swarming about.)

Sure there are some annoying flies in your life. You don't even have to be king (or queen) of the jungle to have some professional annoyers around you. But, along with your annoying folks, your Heavenly Father has added some affirming friends to the mix.

Aren't you glad?

When Paul the apostle sent word from prison to the Christians in Ephesus, he sent it by *FriendEX*. "Tychicus, the dear brother and faithful servant in the Lord, will tell you everything, so that you also may know how I am and what I am doing. I am sending him to you for this very purpose, that you may know how we are, and that he may encourage you" (Eph. 6:21-22).

Evidently Paul had an affirming friend, even in enemy territory. A Spirit-appointed ambassador of heaven who, in Paul's words, would "know how I am and what I am doing."

God's timing is perfect. Along with Paul's jail time for crimes he didn't commit, God sent a support team to affirm him and stand with him. Look around you. There will be someone who is willing to help you carry that "pole"—that burden of proof that Christ is supplying your needs.

Caleb had Joshua. He was at the other end of the pole. Those grapes could have been carried alone . . . but God knew that Caleb needed an affirming friend.

THE GRAPES OF ADMINISTRATION

God is not only the Creator but also the Supplier. He has a whole cluster of grapes for you. And His loving assignment is to administer them in your life. Here are a couple of spiritual standouts:

1. Forgiveness. The Lord Jesus Christ has paid your sin debt. "In him we have redemption through his blood, the forgiveness of sins, in accordance with the riches of God's grace" (Eph. 1:7).

One day a Sunday School teacher asked her class, "Can anyone tell me what we must do before we can be forgiven for sin?"

"I know, I know," the little girl in the front row shouted, waving her hand.

"What's that, Peggy?" the teacher acknowledged.

"We gotta sin."

It's true that all have sinned. And like Adam and Eve, the world's first sinners, we deal with the consequences of sin in our lives. But one of the joys of knowing Christ is His forgiveness of sin! The Scripture teaches, "If we confess our sins, he is faithful and just and will forgive us our sins and purify us from all unrighteousness" (1 John 1:9).

2. Peace. God has made it possible for you to walk through the dark shadows of your life with a guiding light shining in your heart. "And the peace of God, which transcends all understanding, will guard your hearts and your minds in Christ Jesus" (Phil. 4:7).

In 1873 a successful businessman named Horatio Spafford lost his earthly goods in the Chicago fire. Spafford weathered that storm reasoning that his true treasure was in heaven. Just a few weeks later his wife and four children sailed for France on the *Ville du Havre*. He was to join them a short time later. During the Atlantic crossing, the *Ville du Havre* was rammed by an English vessel and sank. Two hundred twenty-six souls were lost, including the Spafford children.

Spafford was given the news while he was crossing the same ocean and was shown the very spot in the Atlantic where his four children met their fate. Although stricken with grief, Spafford looked to the Lord for strength and began to feel a supernatural peace. He recorded that experience in the words of a hymn, now familiar to many who have encountered some troubling times:

> *When peace like a river attendeth my way,*
> *when sorrows like sea billows roll;*

Whatever my lot, Thou has taught me to say,
It is well, it is well with my soul.

Isaiah the prophet put it this way: "You will keep in perfect peace him whose mind is steadfast, because he trusts in you" (Isa. 26:3). The apostle Paul agrees: "Therefore, since we have been made right in God's sight by faith, we have peace with God because of what Jesus Christ our Lord has done for us" (Rom. 5:1, NLT).

THE GRAPES OF PROTECTION

It bears repeating, "He will command his angels concerning you to guard you in all your ways" (Ps. 91:11). Notice that angel is plural. Why send just one angel when a company of angels has already gone through basic training, and they're ready for an assignment!

Scripture is filled with God's promises of lavish protection. Here are just a few of the ways that *He will keep* you!

He will keep you as the apple of His eye. "Keep me as the apple of your eye; hide me in the shadow of your wings" (Ps. 17:8).

He will keep what you have committed to Him. "I know whom I have believed, and am convinced that he is able to guard what I have entrusted to him for that day" (2 Tim. 1:12).

He will keep you as a shepherd cares for his sheep. "Hear the word of the LORD, O nations; proclaim it in distant coastlands: 'He who scattered Israel will gather them and will watch over his flock like a shepherd'" (Jer. 31:10).

He will keep you when you are tempted and when you face trials. "No temptation has seized you except what is common to man. And God is faithful; he will not let you be tempted beyond what you can bear. But when you are tempted, he will also provide a way out so that you can stand up under it" (1 Cor. 10:13).

He will keep you from falling. "To him who is able to keep you from falling and to present you before his glorious presence without fault and with great joy" (Jude 24).

God supplies lavishly. My friend Dr. Jim Diehl defines grace: "Grace is God's special favor freely given to undeserving people."

But what happens when the supply train seems to have been sidetracked?

Noted Southern Gospel singer Vestal Goodman was performing a concert on a day that threatened rain. She led the audience in prayer, asking that God would delay the downpour. Suddenly it began to thunder, lightning flashed across the sky, and a pouring rain soon began to blow across the stage.

Vestal cried out, "Good Lord, people, He said no! Run for cover."

Sometimes He says no. Or at least, not now. The clock of heaven keeps perfect time. God knows *what* we need, *when* we need it, and *how* it should be delivered.

You're bound to get out of sync with God's time once in awhile. You'd hardly be human if you didn't. But, rain or shine, God is in control. Focus on the Rainmaker, not on the rain.

And don't worry about those discussions with Him. That's a sign of your humanity as well. God still paints sunsets—and He still lights the sunrise. He is in control, and don't you forget it! The battle is already won. Hang on to that fact.

It's true that you sometimes feel like you have the spiritual stature (and stamina) of a grasshopper. But "God is great, and God is good." He not only accompanies you through the annoying, troubling times of your life but equips you for them as well.

THE GRAPES OF PLENTY

Painful land or promised land. Either place is a place of God's abundance. Yes, it would be easier to sit under the warm rays of the sun without worrying about the flies. But Adam's first sin added the critters.

Now, we simply have to trust the Master. Jesus is the Friend that stays by us. He forgives us. He guides us. He loves us. And someday soon, He will take us to a better place.

Don't Wait for Your Ship to Come In—
Swim Out to Meet It!
(Turning to Jesus in Troubling Times)

Brother Johnson was a pillar of his church in Kentucky.
He had total faith in God. He lived in a house by a
great river. One night there was a terrible flood. Suddenly he
was standing in river up to his knees. Some men from his
church came by in a boat to rescue him and said, "Get in,
Brother Johnson."

"Oh no," Brother Johnson replied, "I have faith that God
will rescue me."

The water kept rising. Pretty soon Brother Johnson had to
climb up on the roof of his house to escape being drowned. In
a few minutes, a fire department crew came by in another boat
to rescue him, but he refused, "I have faith that God will rescue
me."

A few hours later, he was in river up to his neck. With one
hand he desperately clung to the tip of a TV antenna, and with

flew over, and one of the crew members let down a rope ladder, but Brother Johnson just waved them away, alternately dog-paddling, treading water, and shouting, "I have faith that God will rescue me."

At last, the force of the water broke up the house, and Brother Johnson swam through the Pearly Gates. In heaven, he saw the Lord and commented, "Sir, with all due respect, that last incident was a little embarrassing. I had such faith in You, and told all those rescue people how You were going to save me. Now here I am. Why did You let me drown? Why?"

The story has it that the Lord addressed Brother Johnson's comments rather sternly, "Let you drown? I sent you two bass boats and a traffic helicopter."

Top Ten Things Overheard at the Pearly Gates

10. "No, they're not named after Bill Gates' mom."
 9. "I thought for sure it wasn't loaded."
 8. "I knew I shouldn't have ordered the meat loaf at Denny's."
 7. "Could I see your supervisor?"
 6. "I tried to tell 'em I was sick."
 5. "But, I went to church at Christmas and Easter."
 4. "If I'd known it was going to be this good, I'd have eaten bacon instead of branflakes."
 3. "Listen, Pete, there could be a big tip in this for ya."
 2. "This is a lot better than Indianapolis."
 1. "Is that your final answer?"

God doesn't always answer our prayers the way we expect Him to. But He does answer. To have faith and trust God means that we recognize His activity in our lives, regardless of how hopeless things seem. In our eyes, things may look like they're getting worse instead of better. But be assured, God is at work in our lives. And that is the promise of Rom. 8:28, *And we know that in all things God works for the good of those who love him.*

Here is another glimpse of Jesus at work.

In the course of his journey through Galilee, he arrived at the town of Cana, where he had turned the water into wine. There was a government official in the city of Capernaum whose son was very sick. When he heard that Jesus had come from Judea and was traveling in Galilee, he went over to Cana. He found Jesus and begged him to come to Capernaum with him to heal his son, who was about to die.

Jesus asked, "Must I do miraculous signs and wonders before you people will believe in me?"

The official pleaded, "Lord, please come now before my little boy dies."

Then Jesus told him, "Go back home. Your son will live!" And the man believed Jesus' word and started home *(John 4:46-50, NLT).*

I'm reminded of another incident on the high seas. The disciples were out in their fishing boat when a severe storm came up. One of the disciples, Peter, spotted Jesus walking on the water toward the troubled crew. Peter got a glimpse of the Master, threw off his coat, jumped into the waves, and headed toward Him.

Now, he didn't make it all the way to Jesus. He got to thinking about the waves instead of the Wave Walker and swallowed a good portion of the lake. But he was headed in the right direction: away from the problem and toward the Problem Solver.

You may say, "I'm not very good with directions." Maybe not. Maybe you need a road map to get back to your room after getting a drink of water during the night. But one thing I do know, if you're going through troubling times, it's best to head straight for Jesus.

The nobleman of this story did. He was a court official in Herod's government and possibly even one of Herod's relatives, and his son was sick. All human efforts had failed. Jesus, the Great Physician, was his last (and best) hope. Position or influence didn't matter now. The only thing that mattered was that little boy lying on the cot near death.

Let's take a closer look at this incident. It has some important truths. The actions and attitudes of the royal official offer us some real insights into dealing with our troubling times.

He Went to the Right Source

"When he heard that Jesus had come from Judea and was traveling in Galilee, he went over to Cana."

This wasn't the time for a call to some fake fortune-teller on late-night TV. This wasn't the time to seek some 16-year-old swami or some geriatric guru. This wasn't a time for home remedies. The little boy needed a heavenly remedy.

This wasn't even the time for a theological debate over how many angels would fit on the tip of a pin. This was a time for personal faith in a personal God.

Some folks say they believe in God, but they believe in an abstract way. Their faith isn't personal. They'll *say* that He is a God of miracles, but their actions contradict their words.

A classic sermon illustration points that out. A famous tightrope walker once stretched a rope across the thunderous Niagara Falls. While the breathless audience looked on, he carefully inched his way across to the other side. Then he took his performance to the next level. He took his careful journey back—blindfolded. The crowd cheered. Sensing their amazement, the tightrope walker—still blindfolded—pushed a specially made wheelbarrow across the expanse.

The crowds went wild. Standing on the perch at the end of the tightrope, the aerialist waited for the cheering to stop. Then he shouted to them, "Does anyone here believe I can push a man in this wheelbarrow across the falls?"

A gentleman in the front waved his hands, shouting, "I do. I believe."

"Then," said the walker, "come on up here. Get into the wheelbarrow, and let me push you across the falls."

To nobody's surprise, the man's intellectual assent failed to translate into personal belief. (That's the uptown way of saying he chickened out.) The wheelbarrow stood empty as the man slouched his way out of the crowd.

Troubling times call for more than mental assent. They call for personal belief. And they call for faith-filled action.

You see, it's one thing to believe that Jesus the Creator can work miracles. It's quite another to make it a personal commitment—to bring your miracle-needing trouble to Him.

He Had the Right Attitude

The father put all of his pomp and circumstance aside when he reached Jesus. The Scripture says he "begged him to come to Capernaum with him to heal his son, who was about to die."

This wasn't the time to brag about his connections, to let everyone know that he was related to Herod. This wasn't the time to boast about his contribution to the United Way. This wasn't the time to bring out that framed sheepskin with the official looking alphabet letters and dots behind his name.

This wasn't the time to have people autograph his baptism certificate. This wasn't the time to display the digital photo of that brass nameplate on the church pew (the one he had given as a memorial to himself).

A little boy was sick—his little boy. And Jesus was the best (and only) source for a miracle recovery.

I'm reminded of another royal incident—this one in the life of an Old Testament army commander who had leprosy and needed a miracle. It's worth a read:

> Now Naaman was commander of the army of the king of Aram. He was a great man in the sight of his master and highly regarded, because through him the LORD had given victory to Aram. He was a valiant soldier, but he had leprosy.
>
> Now bands from Aram had gone out and had taken captive a young girl from Israel, and she served Naaman's wife. She said to her mistress, "If only my master would see the prophet who is in Samaria! He would cure him of his leprosy."
>
> Naaman went to his master and told him what the girl from Israel had said. "By all means, go," the king of Aram replied. "I will send a letter to the king of Israel." So Naaman left, taking with him ten talents of silver, six thousand shekels of gold and ten sets of clothing. The letter that he took to the king of Israel read: "With this letter I am sending my servant Naaman to you so that you may cure him of his leprosy."
>
> As soon as the king of Israel read the letter, he tore his robes and said, "Am I God? Can I kill and bring back to life?

Why does this fellow send someone to me to be cured of his leprosy? See how he is trying to pick a quarrel with me!"

When Elisha the man of God heard that the king of Israel had torn his robes, he sent him this message: "Why have you torn your robes? Have the man come to me and he will know that there is a prophet in Israel." So Naaman went with his horses and chariots and stopped at the door of Elisha's house. Elisha sent a messenger to say to him, "Go, wash yourself seven times in the Jordan, and your flesh will be restored and you will be cleansed."

But Naaman went away angry and said, "I thought that he would surely come out to me and stand and call on the name of the LORD his God, wave his hand over the spot and cure me of my leprosy. Are not Abana and Pharpar, the rivers of Damascus, better than any of the waters of Israel? Couldn't I wash in them and be cleansed?" So he turned and went off in a rage.

Naaman's servants went to him and said, "My father, if the prophet had told you to do some great thing, would you not have done it? How much more, then, when he tells you, 'Wash and be cleansed'!" So he went down and dipped himself in the Jordan seven times, as the man of God had told him, and his flesh was restored and became clean like that of a young boy *(2 Kings 5:1-14)*.

Poor Naaman. There he stood with sores all over his skin, having a royal hissy over doing what the prophet of God, Elisha, said to do to be free from his leprosy.

"I'm not going to dip my royal robes in that muddy Jordan River!"

"Doesn't that Elisha guy know who I am?"

† 75

Sure, Elisha knew who he was. But he also knew what he had—leprosy. And he knew there was only one cure: God's cure. This wasn't a time for mind games. This was a time to dip some pride in the Jordan.

Not just the right source but also the right attitude. If you're in troubling times, it's time to run to Jesus with a believing heart and a humble dependence.

The royal official whose son was sick had the right attitude. He begged Him to come and heal his son.

He Made the Right Demands

Whoa! Demands? I hear you: "Didn't you just say that turning to Jesus in troubling times called for an attitude of humility? And now you're talking demands."

John Bisango describes a time when his five-year-old daughter, Melodye Jan, came to him and asked for a dollhouse. John promptly nodded and promised to build her one, then he went back to reading his book. Soon he glanced out the study window and saw her arms filled with dishes, toys, and dolls, making trip after trip until she had a great pile of playthings in the yard. He asked his wife what Melodye Jan was doing.

"Oh, you promised to build her a dollhouse, and she believes you. She's just getting ready for it."

"You would have thought I'd been hit by an atom bomb," John later said. "I threw aside that book, raced to the lumber yard for supplies, and quickly built that little girl a dollhouse. Now, why did I respond? Because I wanted to? No. Because she deserved it? No. Her daddy had given his word, and she believed it and acted upon it. When I saw her faith, nothing could keep me from carrying out my word."[1]

Notice what the royal official said to Jesus in response to

His chastisement over wholesale miracle-seeking: "'Unless you people see miraculous signs and wonders,' Jesus told him, 'you will never believe.' The royal official said, 'Sir, come down before my child dies.'"

Sounds pretty demanding, doesn't it?

It was. This was a desperate situation. The little boy was in trouble—and that troubled a devoted father.

Jesus had the cure and time was running out. This called for a bold move.

It wasn't the only bold move recorded in the Bible. Look at this incident:

Leaving that place, Jesus withdrew to the region of Tyre and Sidon. A Canaanite woman from that vicinity came to him, crying out, "Lord, Son of David, have mercy on me! My daughter is suffering terribly from demon-possession."

Jesus did not answer a word. So his disciples came to him and urged him, "Send her away, for she keeps crying out after us."

He answered, "I was sent only to the lost sheep of Israel."

The woman came and knelt before him. "Lord, help me!" she said.

He replied, "It is not right to take the children's bread and toss it to their dogs."

"Yes, Lord," she said, "but even the dogs eat the crumbs that fall from their masters' table."

Then Jesus answered, "Woman, you have great faith! Your request is granted." And her daughter was healed from that very hour *(Matt. 15:21-28)*.

The Canaanite woman dared to debate the Master. Why? She was desperate—and her daughter was in trouble.

God is big enough to withstand our demands.

Jesus taught that. "So I tell you to ask and you will receive, search and you will find, knock and the door will be opened for you. Everyone who asks will receive, everyone who searches will find, and the door will be opened for everyone who knocks" (Luke 11:9-10).

Every step, from the first ask to the last knock, was a demanding one. Jesus taught us that it's all right to seek Him with persistence—to make demands on His wonderful mercy and grace. Remember the words of the writer to the Hebrews? "Anyone who comes to him must believe that he exists and that he rewards those who earnestly seek him" (11:6).

Charles Wesley wrote: "Faith, mighty faith, the promise sees, and looks to that alone; Laughs at life's impossibilities, And cries, 'It shall be done!'"

He Made the Right Decision

When it was all said and done, the official had done everything God said to do. "Jesus replied, 'You may go, your son will live.' The man took Jesus at his word and departed." It may be the best advice you ever receive—especially when you're going through troubling times: Take God at His word.

The Bible—the Word of God—is the best first-aid handbook ever written. In it, there's a promise for every pain or every problem. Your troubling times may exhaust you, but they'll never exhaust the help and healing of God's Word. The psalmist had that in mind as he sat reading his devotions. "The law of the LORD is perfect, reviving the soul. The statutes of the LORD are trustworthy, making wise the simple. The precepts of the LORD are right, giving joy to the heart. The commands of the LORD are radiant, giving light to the eyes" (Ps. 19:7-8).

Reviving. Trustworthy. Wisdom-giving. Joy-giving. Enlightening. It's simply best to take God at His word.

Top Ten Signs You're Not Reading Your Bible Enough

10. You think Abraham, Isaac, and Jacob were a rock group from the '60s.

9. You think the Epistles were the wives of the apostles.

8. You think the minor prophets discovered coal.

7. You fall for it when the Sunday School teacher says, "Turn to the Book of Hesitations."

6. You don't swallow that story about Jonah and the whale.

5. Field mice have taken up residence in your family Bible.

4. You have to look in the table of contents to find the Book of Genesis.

3. You look for speakers to plug in the *Amplified Bible*.

2. You blow the dust off it, and it sends your cat into an asthmatic attack.

1. It's still shrink-wrapped.

Jacqueline was an elderly woman who lived to take care of her wheelchair-bound daughter. When her daughter died, Jacqueline lost not only her purpose for living but also her living companion. Her cottage in the country seemed as empty as an eggshell. Occasionally a friend called or a note arrived, but most of her time was spent in oppressive, ongoing solitude. Her health didn't allow her to circulate very much, and her best friends were now all in heaven.

One day, Jacqueline's Bible opened to Phil. 4:5 and four words struck her forcefully: "The Lord is near." "If so," thought Jacqueline, "I should be more aware of it."

"Lord," she said, "I'm going to pretend You're here all the time. No, forgive me for using that word; there is no pretending to be done. I'm going to use my God-given imagination to visualize how very present You really are. Help me to ever *re-mind myself* of the reality of Your nearness."

That evening as she retired, she said, "I'm going on to bed now, Lord. Will You please watch over me as I sleep?" The next morning on awakening, she said, "Good morning, Lord. This is the day You have made." Sitting down with her hot tea, she read through the Book of Philippians again, underlining verse 5, then she prayed aloud for a very long time. At noon, she said, "Now, Lord, let's watch the news on television, so You can show me things in this world I can pray for." Jacqueline and the Lord watched the news together, then she prayed for flood victims in the Delta, a newly installed president in an African country, and for a man sentenced to life imprisonment.

At supper, she bowed her head and thanked the Lord for her food, but she didn't feel her prayers were traveling up to heaven. She felt instead that she was talking to someone sitting across the table from her.

Gradually her attitude was transformed. The loneliness lessened, her joy increased, her fears diminished, and she never afterward felt she was alone in the house. Jacqueline was learning how to abide in the Presence.[2]

But there's something else about the official's actions and attitude that we should note.

He Gave the Right Witness

His actions and reactions to God's miracle-working power influenced others. "While he was still on the way, his servants met him with the news that his boy was living. When he inquired as to the time when his son got better, they said to him, 'The fever left him yesterday at the seventh hour.' Then the father realized that this was the exact time at which Jesus had said to him, 'Your son will live.' So he and all his household believed" (John 4:51-54).

Notice: "This was the exact time." What time? God's time. (He's always on time.)

The father left Jesus with a miracle in his heart. He hadn't seen it yet. He didn't know what the packaging would look like. But he knew that Jesus would work it out—in His own time! You just can't keep a faith like that to yourself!

The Philippian jailer didn't. New Testament leaders Paul and Silas were thrown into jail for telling people the truth about God's love and forgiveness (what a horrible crime). Instead of whining about their fate, they held a concert. And all heaven broke loose (Acts 16).

The prison was shaken. The prison doors opened. The jailer woke up. (Well, duh.)

Paul and Silas had an opportunity to tell the miracle story of their release. It didn't take long for the jailer to realize that he wanted a piece of *that* pie.

> The jailer called for lights, rushed in and fell trembling before Paul and Silas. He then brought them out and asked, "Sirs, what must I do to be saved?" They replied, "Believe in the Lord Jesus, and you will be saved—you and your household." Then they spoke the word of the Lord to him and to all the others in his house. At that hour of the night the jailer took them and washed their wounds; then immediately he and all his family were baptized *(Acts 16:29-33)*.

Did you notice it? "At that hour of the night." God is always on time!

His turning to Jesus influenced the jailer's household.

81

That's always true. You can't make a move toward the Master without somebody catching it on the tape of his or her heart. A Sunday School teacher asked her class, "Why do you believe in God?" In reporting some of the answers, the teacher confessed that the one she liked best came from a boy who said, "I don't know. I guess it's just something that runs in the family."

What a great story, and a true one at that. An official of Herod's government had a dying son that needed a miracle. The official made all the right moves: He went to the right source. He had the right attitude. He made the right decision. He made the right demands. He gave the right witness.

And there was a happy ending: The boy was healed.

But I've been a pastor long enough to know that all the endings aren't that happy. Sometimes there isn't a healing. Sometimes there is a sad farewell. Sometimes you and I can do everything by the book and still end up with a bucketful of tears and a floor littered with shattered dreams.

What are we to do? Just keep trusting God. Be quick to run to Him. He's the source of your help. Cast your calendar at His feet and let Him write in or edit the events according to His loving purpose. He has not failed you before. And He will not fail you now. You can turn to Him in the troubling times of your life.

Don't wait for your ship to come in—swim out to meet it.

---

1. John Bisango, *The Power of Positive Praying* (Grand Rapids: Zondervan, 1965), 24.

2. Robert Hall Glover, *The Bible Basis of Missions* (Chicago: Moody Press, 1946), 56.

Don't Wait for the Hearse
to Take You to Church
(Discovering Your Spiritual Self)

I heard about a man who was extremely proud of the things he owned. But his most prized possession was his car, a brand-new Jaguar. Loaded with more options than a menu in a Chinese restaurant, the automobile was the envy of his friends (and a couple of relatives). The car had become the central thing in his life. In fact, he put a clause in his will that in the event of his death, he would be buried in that car. (Probably making it quite difficult to line up any pallbearers.)

The dreaded day arrived, and his last wishes were carried out.

At the cemetery, one of his envious friends watched as his buddy was lowered into the grave, car and all, and he was overcome with emotion. "Man," he exclaimed, "that's really living!"

Millions of people are searching for meaning in life, and often in the process they attach themselves to things that won't last. Money is soon spent. Possessions wear out. Even relation-ships lose their appeal.

In the end, like the man in the Jaguar, they are disappointed to find that what they thought would be "really living" is sim-ply another sad way to die.

William James said that the greatest use of life is to spend it for something that will outlast it. How true. And Jesus Christ provides that. He is the way, the truth, and the life—the only one who can bring both meaning to life and victory over death.

It's interesting to note that real meaning in life comes from something "out of this world." Spiritual. Eternal. A right rela-tionship to God and a hope for the future are at the core of contented living.

And the answer is not that far away. I believe that we have an *inner religion,* so to speak. We are born with a desire to have a relationship with an eternal God. And the discovery (or redis-covery) of that relationship helps put all the puzzle pieces of life together. Someone asked pastor and author Leith Anderson this question, "If you could say one sentence to a secular audience, what would you say?" Anderson responded with this: "You matter to God."

Let me illustrate. Children don't have to be taught to love God. We don't have to force them to sing "Jesus loves me this I know, for the Bible tells me so." They love to sing it—because they have a natural love for God. John Wesley said that there was a divine stamp on our hearts.

Not loving God is a learned behavior. Rebelling against Him takes practice. The tendency is there because we inherited it from our forefather, Adam. Rom. 5:12 says, "Sin entered the world through one man, and death through sin." Death, spiri-tual separation from God, is the result of disobeying God. Oswald Chambers said, "The essence of sin is the refusal to recognize we are accountable to God at all."

Now, before we get buried in three layers of theology, let's just say that God desires a spiritual relationship with us and we have a natural *want-to* to be a part of it. It's a relationship for these times—especially for these times.

Standing amid the rubble near Ground Zero in New York City was a two-century-old building: a church. Covered with dust and ashes, unmoved by the terrorist attacks on the World Trade Center, it became a shelter for rescue workers and displaced persons. Symbolic? Of course. But a relationship with God is more than a church building. It comes before church membership (or church attendance).

Personal faith in Jesus Christ is Christianity. It's not memorizing a set of rules, sitting in a certain church auditorium seat, giving a certain amount to the cathedral coffers. It's not singing in the choir or sitting on the deacon board. It's not being in the Missionary Circle or the Men's Bowling League. It's all about being related to God through personal faith in His Son. "To all who received him, to those who believed in his name, he gave the right to become children of God" (John 1:12). Now don't get me wrong. I've been the pastor of a church for a long time. And I won't discourage attending church, giving in the offering, singing in the choir, or joining the Missionary Circle. If you have the desire to do any of that, please be my guest. But the fact is, that's not what you're looking for. Until you find Christ—until you've surrendered the emptiness of your life to His forgiveness and fullness, you can't say, "Man, that's really living."

God is on time. He has perfect faith in you, and you can have perfect faith in Him, for a time like this. Spirituality has never been obsolete, but it seems to be more in fashion these days.

Tough times often bring that on. Ann Graham Lotz, gifted author, speaker, and daughter of Dr. Billy Graham, was interviewed on a morning news TV program. The host rather cynically asked her where God was during the September 11, 2001, attack on the United States. Her answer was terrific. She told the host that God was a perfect gentleman. He didn't usually go where He was not welcome. She reminded that dazed host that God had been left off the invitation to our courts, our schools, our businesses, and our homes. Now, suddenly He was welcome.

But there is an eager search for personal faith. One newspaper account told of the CEO and some other executives of a large corporation who put their business plan on a table along with the sales forecasts and their tepid financial reports. Then they joined hands around the table and prayed for God's help in their business. That's not only a miracle event in the corporate world but also a miracle that made the newspapers.

"God Bless America" is suddenly the banner of choice, whether it's on the bumper of a Ford or on the wall of a financial institution. But what does it mean to have a personal and confident faith in God? And why shouldn't we wait for the hearse to take us to church?

Let's understand several important things about having a personal faith in God—about discovering your spiritual self.

"He has made everything beautiful in its time. He has also set eternity in the hearts of men; yet they cannot fathom what God has done from beginning to end" (Eccles. 3:11).

IT'S FACTORY INSTALLED

You're going to worship something. If it's not God, it might be your geraniums. You were born with an inner desire to worship. Now when I say worship, I'm not talking about standing on your aching feet during the half-hour of praise and worship in your local church. (I'm a fan of praise and worship. But sometimes I fear that it's possible to stand on your feet so long during the singing that some parishioner on his or her last leg could pass away from sheer exhaustion. And no one would notice until the praise team had packed away the microphones and turned off the PowerPoint.)

I'm not talking about reciting rosaries or singing praise choruses. I'm talking about the natural tendency to express worthship (which is what worship is all about)—something your inner self is already comfortable with. It may not be focused on God. It may be focused on family, fortunes, or football, but it's there. The apostle Paul illustrated that during a Bible-times missionary tour in Greece. Spotting religious symbols, signs, and statues all around him, he addressed the "religion" of his audience.

Paul then stood up in the meeting of the Areopagus and said: "Men of Athens! I see that in every way you are very religious. For as I walked around and looked carefully at your objects of worship, I even found an altar with this inscription: TO AN UNKNOWN GOD. Now what you worship as something unknown I am going to proclaim to you.

The God who made the world and everything in it is the Lord of heaven and earth and does not live in temples built by hands. And he is not served by human hands, as if he needed anything, because he himself gives all men life and breath and everything else. From one man he made every nation of men, that they should inhabit the whole earth; and he determined the times set for them and the exact places where they should live. God did this so that men would seek him and perhaps reach out for him and find him, though he is not far from each one of us. "For in him we live and move and have our being." As some of your own poets have said, "We are his offspring."

Therefore since we are God's offspring, we should not think that the divine being is like gold or silver or stone—an image made by man's design and skill *(Acts 17:22-29).*

Paul made an eloquent pitch for real-time religion. He wasn't inviting people to cold statues and hollow temples. He was inviting folks to snuggle up spiritually to a warmhearted God who cared enough about them to sacrifice His only Son. He wanted them to move out of a "religion" into a "relationship."

There's something else you ought to know about this personal faith.

IT'S BETTER *FOUND* THAN *FORCED*

When I was a child, we couldn't afford uptown spinach. I was raised on down-home "manna from heaven": green beans. Now friends, give me a quarter-plate full of West Virginia green beans, swimming in bacon grease (for sure, its not on the popular South Beach Diet!) and then set a slice of warm cornbread beside a healthy portion of fried potatoes on the same plate and I'm telling you, *it's a spiritual experience.*

Green beans or spinach, not everyone liked them when they were forced on them. But later on, when those same folks learned how good they tasted when they're anointed with grease and positioned on the dinner plate, they made a personal discovery. Found is better than forced.

I heard one ol' boy say that he had a *drug* problem when he was a child. His parents *drug* him to Sunday School, *drug* him to church, and *drug* him to the midweek service. You may have been *drugged* as a child (and I'm not talking about Ritalin). Faith may have been forced on you—and maybe it didn't take. If so, there's a whole new, exciting world out there.

Faith that is found is personal and powerful. When you discover on your own that God loves you for who you are and not for someone you're supposed to be, you will be liberated.

It's Best When It's Focused on Christ

Jesus spelled it out to one of His disciples clearly enough for a kindergarten student to understand on the opening day of school.

> Jesus said to his disciples, "Don't be worried! Have faith in God and have faith in me. There are many rooms in my Father's house. I wouldn't tell you this, unless it was true. I am going there to prepare a place for each of you. After I have done this, I will come back and take you with me. Then we will be together. You know the way to where I am going."
>
> Thomas said, "Lord, we don't even know where you are going! How can we know the way?"
>
> "I am the way, the truth, and the life!" Jesus answered. "Without me, no one can go to the Father. If you had known me, you would have known the Father. But from now on, you do know him, and you have seen him" *(John 14:1-7, CEV)*.

Did you notice? *Many rooms* but one *way*. I know that's pretty narrow thinking in a time when you can't even talk about a manhole cover in the street without changing its gender reference, but I believe it because it's Bible. Rom. 3:20-24 says:

> No one will be declared righteous in his sight by ob-

serving the law; rather, through the law we become conscious of sin. But now a righteousness from God, apart from law, has been made known, to which the Law and the Prophets testify. This righteousness from God comes through faith in Jesus Christ to all who believe. There is no difference, for all have sinned and fall short of the glory of God, and are justified freely by his grace through the redemption that came by Christ Jesus.

God's only Son, the Lord Jesus Christ, is our source of "right-ness" (righteousness). When you make that discovery and put down that stake in God's territory, you won't have to wait for a hearse to take you to church.

There's something else about a personal faith in God that you're invited to understand.

It Makes a Better Verb than It Does Noun

Recently I thought back over the years of elementary school, high school, and college, and thought about all those English lessons. You know, in all my years of writing and speaking, in all my years of leading churches, in all my years of training pastors and laypersons—in all those years, not one person has asked me for a counseling appointment to discuss the proper use of nouns and verbs.

But there *is* a difference. And it can even be seen in our religion. Nouns are something you are, a place you've been, or something you're making the payments on. A verb is something that's in process. It's an action. Some folks see religion as a noun. They bought it (so they think) and now they're displaying it on a shelf, like a nine-year-old Nativity set from that oversized aunt that's always hugging them and pinching their cheeks.

Others see their religion as a verb. It's active. There isn't any dust on it. It's always fresh. In the words of the hymn writer, "Morning by morning, new mercies I see." It's as alive to them as the Christ they serve. That's exciting personal faith.

IT'S FUN

I'll never understand why faith-based living is viewed as something akin to a root canal. I've had the time of my life serving Jesus! And even the *worst times* have been times of inner joy. Knowing that you're forgiven—knowing that you are accepted by God, even when the Pharisees launch an offensive against you, is enough to put a smile on your face.

If you're going to "get religion," you might as well get one with the batteries included. You might as well enjoy it.

Personal faith in God has an additional benefit.

IT'S AS MUCH OF A PREVENTION AS IT IS CURE

During the anthrax scare that followed the attack on America, people were forced to take antibiotics as a preventative measure as well as a cure. A personal faith is like that. It not only cures but also keeps. The apostle Peter wrote about that in his letter to Christians:

Praise be to the God and Father of our Lord Jesus Christ! In his great mercy he has given us new birth into a living hope through the resurrection of Jesus Christ from the dead, and into an inheritance that can never perish, spoil or fade—kept in heaven for you, who through faith are shielded by God's power until the coming of the salvation that is ready to be revealed in the last time *(1 Pet. 1:3-5)*.

A personal faith in God isn't just about *not doing things*. It's also about doing the right things—the things that bring inner peace and outer influence for Christ. I've known folks who thought they could be happy by *giving up* this or that. But when it was self-motivated, the more they gave up the emptier they felt. Nothing plus nothing equals what? They looked (and acted) like they had swallowed a hand grenade with the pin pulled.

And I've known folks who have made some personal sacrifices based solely on what they believed to be God's will for their lives. And the sacrifices turned into a bonus. You can spot them in the crowd. They have more joy about them than a room full of puppies.

When you make life choices based on the direction of God's Spirit and the instruction of His Word, you're not a *victim* of life you're its *victor.* The psalmist talked about the safety of his personal relationship with God. "If the LORD delights in a man's way, he makes his steps firm; though he stumble, he will not fall, for the LORD upholds him with his hand" (Ps. 37:23-24).

IT'S EVEN BETTER WHEN THINGS GET WORSE

You remember that wedding reception in Cana. The host remarked, "You have saved the best until last." That's what a personal relationship with God through faith in Jesus Christ is like. It just keeps getting better, even when there's a cloud cover.

Personal faith in God is fireproof. That doesn't mean we won't suffer some scorches and burns. But the Bible says that heaven's fire extinguisher will keep us safe when we walk obediently and in confidence. Eph. 6:16: "In addition to all this, take up the shield of faith, with which you can extinguish all the flaming arrows of the evil one."

God has saved the best for last. Heaven will replace the horrors. His children may have little here, but they'll have plenty there. There may be tears here, but there'll be triumph there. There may be pain here, but there'll be comfort there.

Death awaits us here—life awaits us there.

Good-bye is common here—hello is common there.

We *believe* here—we'll *see* there.

The wisdom writer summed it up: "The path of the righteous is like the first gleam of dawn, shining ever brighter till the full light of day" (Prov. 4:18).

In 1997, more than 1 million men gathered in one of the most historic meetings of modern times. The Washington, D.C., "Stand in the Gap" rally of the Promise Keepers organization brought together men from every denomination and walk of life.

Several outstanding speakers presented the message of Christ to live a life of holiness in their homes and in their places of employment. And when the invitations were given, thousands of them answered the call of commitment.

One of the speakers was well-known author Max Lucado. In making his point about the single source of our salvation, he asked the men to shout out the names of the denomination with which they were associated.

Almost like rolling thunder, the names of the denominations were shouted. The jumble of names was massive and very confusing, as you can imagine.

Then, Lucado quieted the men and asked them to shout the name of their Savior. Those who were there will never forget it. Over 1 million men shouted in one voice, *Jesus!*

They got the message.

Church affiliation alone isn't the answer. *Jesus* is the answer. "Salvation is found in no one else, for there is no other name under heaven given to men by which we must be saved" (Acts 4:12). A personal relationship with God through faith in His Son, the Lord Jesus Christ, is God's on-time answer for your life and mine.

Grab for All the Gusto Before You Die
(Growing at God's Pace)

I spend a lot of time in airplanes, often flying into Dallas on my way back home to Oklahoma. (You can't go anywhere from Oklahoma unless you go through Dallas first. When you die in Oklahoma, it doesn't matter if you are going to heaven or hell—you go to Dallas first.)

It's amazing to me how far into the distance you can see from 33,000 feet in the air. Coming in from California, the pilot pointed out that the lights we were seeing in the distance from the left side of the airplane was Oklahoma City—where I live—nearly 400 miles away. I was amazed how far out I was seeing.

How I would love to be lifted up 33,000 feet above my life. Then I could see into the future. Then I would know just what God has in store for me tomorrow, next week, next month, the rest of my life.

But that isn't how God does it. He does not tell us what is

going to happen tomorrow—only that He will still be with us tomorrow.

But that is usually not enough for us. We want to live life in the fast-forward mode. We aren't satisfied with where we are today. We think that tomorrow will bring us all we want to be ultimately happy.

Too many times we who profess faith in the on-time God don't see Him moving fast enough, so we put our own plans in action.

Instead of waiting for God to lead us to the right job, we spend hours surfing monstrously hot Internet job sites.

We're tired of driving a perfectly good three-year-old car, so we go deeper in debt to get the latest and greatest.

We haven't met the perfect mate, so we settle for someone with no social graces and—worst of all—no relationship with God.

If you see yourself in any of the above, you are in good company. Abraham couldn't wait for God either, so he took matters in his owns hands. You remember when Abraham was still known as Abram? And the night that God led him outside his tent to look at the sky, He told Abram, "Look up into the heavens and count the stars if you can. Your descendants will be like that—too many to count!" (Gen. 15:5, NLT).

But Abram grew tired of waiting for God to fulfill His end of the deal. So when Sarai (later called Sarah) offered Abram her maid as a surrogate mother, Abram sidestepped God and created his own descendant. The problem was that Ishmael, the son born to Abram and Sarai's maid, Hagar, was not the heir God wanted to build His people through. As a matter of fact, Ishmael is the ancestor of the modern-day Muslims. Can you see how working outside of God's time frame can have long-lasting, devastating results?

Another man who tried to do it his way was Achan. He was an Israelite who marched across the Jordan River with Joshua to inherit the joys of the Promised Land, just as God had promised. (You may recall the land of the giant grapes I mentioned in chapter 4.) But before Joshua, Achan, and the rest of the Jews could enjoy the milk and honey God promised would be theirs, they had to drive the current residents out and destroy everything. They were not to keep any of the loot from their conquered foes.

Their first stop was Jericho, where the walls came a tumblin' down. There was no stopping the children of Israel now. It looked like it would be a rout—like the New York Yankees playing baseball against a group of sandlot players.

Next up was the town of Ai. The scouting report on this opponent was promising.

"Joshua sent some of his men from Jericho to spy out the city of Ai, east of Bethel, near Beth-aven. When they returned, they told Joshua, 'It's a small town, and it won't take more than two or three thousand of us to destroy it. There's no need for all of us to go there'" (Josh. 7:2-3, NLT).

Piece of cake, Josh. Send in the scrubs and get them some playing time.

But the outcome was a complete upset.

"So approximately three thousand warriors were sent, but they were soundly defeated. The men of Ai chased the Israelites from the city gate as far as the quarries, and they killed about thirty-six who were retreating down the slope. The Israelites were paralyzed with fear at this turn of events, and their courage melted away" (Josh. 7:4-5, NLT).

What happened? How could the team that put a whoopin'
on mighty Jericho suffer such defeat at the hands of tiny Ai?
Joshua called the leaders together and had an all-night prayer
meeting, but God was not pleased.

The LORD said to Joshua, "Get up! Why are you lying
on your face like this? Israel has sinned and broken my
covenant! They have stolen the things that I commanded to
be set apart for me. And they have not only stolen them;
they have also lied about it and hidden the things among
their belongings. That is why the Israelites are running
from their enemies in defeat. For now Israel has been set
apart for destruction. I will not remain with you any longer
unless you destroy the things among you that were set apart
for destruction" *(Josh. 7:10-12, NLT)*.

Wow. Talk about a direct answer. Joshua did not wait a moment. Early in the morning he brought all of Israel before him,
divided into their tribes. He used a special kind of dice that the
priests had to determine God's will, and selected the tribe of Judah. The rest of the tribes could go back to their tents. Then
from the tribe of Judah, the clan of Zerah was chosen. From this
clan the family of Zimri was singled out. Achan could feel the
sweat rolling down his back. Each person from Zimri's family
was brought forward, and Achan was selected as the guilty party.

Then Joshua said to Achan, "My son, give glory to the
LORD, the God of Israel, by telling the truth. Make your
confession and tell me what you have done. Don't hide it
from me."

Achan replied, "I have sinned against the LORD, the
God of Israel. For I saw a beautiful robe imported from
Babylon, two hundred silver coins, and a bar of gold weigh-
ing more than a pound. I wanted them so much that I took

them. They are hidden in the ground beneath my tent, with the silver buried deeper than the rest" *(Josh. 7:19-21, NLT)*.

Achan's end was swift as he and his family were executed and all of their possessions destroyed. The sad thing is, if Achan had been patient God would have gladly blessed him with all of the things he desired and more. God's blessings always come on time—just not always on *our* time.

Are you aching to plan your own future? Join the crowd. Many—if not most—of those around you also long to reach into the future and get to where they're going. Here are a few of the reasons why.

WE WANT THE RESULTS, NOT THE PROCESS

I know many writers who have told me they hate writing but love having written. Writing a book or a magazine article or a letter to a friend or a journal entry is—laborious. It is tedious to come up with all the right words and then get them to fit into a sentence surrounded with the correct punctuation marks. Often I have so many red and green squiggly marks (indicating misspelled words and incorrect grammar) that my computer screen looks like Christmas paper.

But once the book is completed, edited, and printed, it is a wonderful occasion. Actually, it is more of a relief. And then to see the book actually sitting on a shelf in the local megabookstore is a great delight. (Unless it is on the 50-cent bargain rack.)

If I skip the writing process, however, and the book just magically appears on the shelf, would I still feel the joy of accomplishment? No, of course not. We are wired by our Maker to be workers. The result of our labor is our reward. Skipping the process will not get us to the result, at least not the result we want. The process can also be the reward.

WE WANT TO REACH THE DESTINATION, NOT ENJOY THE DRIVE

Are you the kind of driver who piles the family in the SUV, hits the highway, and only stops when the needle on the gas gauge is below E? Or do you take the time to stop at all of the historical markers you pass along the way?

As Christians, our ultimate destination is our eternal home with Christ. But if we were not meant to enjoy our lives here and now, why doesn't God just take us to heaven the day we profess Jesus as our Savior?

God made us to live. Look at just a sampling of God's exhortation to us to live:

"Then the LORD God formed man of dust from the ground, and breathed into his nostrils the breath of life; and man became a living being" (Gen. 2:7, NASB).

"Today I have given you the choice between life and death, between blessings and curses. I call on heaven and earth to witness the choice you make. Oh, that you would choose life, that you and your descendants might live!" (Deut. 30:19, NLT).

"You gave me life and showed me your unfailing love. My life was preserved by your care" (Job 10:12, NLT).

"I came so they can have real and eternal life, more and better life than they ever dreamed of" (John 10:10, TM).

I love the Frank Sinatra song "I'm Gonna Live Till I Die."

> *I'm gonna live till I die,*
> *I'm gonna laugh 'stead of cry,*
> *I gonna take the town,*
> *Turn it upside down.*
> *I'm gonna live, live, live until I die.*

That's how I see life as God has given it to us. He wants us to live now, not just hang on for heaven. Remember, eternal life starts now.

WE DON'T TRUST GOD TO HANDLE OUR TOMORROWS

We started this chapter 33,000 feet in the air on approach to the airport in Dallas/Fort Worth. I was telling you how I could see my hometown 400 miles away. Oh, how I wish I could be lifted up to see where my life is leading. But that is not how God operates.

Why doesn't He? Why doesn't God give us a AAA TripTik to show us exactly where we are going throughout our lives? Because if He did, we would not have to develop our faith in Him.

Paul tells us in Rom. 8:24, "For if you already have something, you don't need to hope for it" (NLT).

Most of us think of the word "hope" in the same way as "wish." "I *hope* he likes me." "I *hope* my team wins." "I *hope* I get a big bonus at work." This is not the original meaning of the word, however. *Hope*'s roots go back to an ancient nautical term that meant "point of destination." Your *hope* is what you are navigating toward. This helps Rom. 8:24 make much more sense, doesn't it? If we already have something, we don't have to plan how to get it. But if we are still waiting, we plan our route to get where we want to be.

Think of your life as a path through dark woods. You have a flashlight to aid your walk. Do you shine it way off into the distance, trying to see where the path is taking you? If so, chances are good that you will stumble over something right at your feet.

If you are smart (which I know you are), you will shine the light so that your next step is sure and firm.

101

The flashlight God has given us for our journey in this life is His Word. Ps. 119:105 tells us (if you are an Amy Grant fan, you can sing this verse), "Thy word is a lamp to my feet, and a light to my path" (NASB). God promises to guide our feet in their next step. We must trust that tomorrow's steps will be just as firm as today's.

TOMORROW IS UNCERTAIN; WE WANT TO KNOW THE OUTCOME TODAY

We have heard that layoffs are imminent.

The admission letter from the college we really want to attend should be here any day now.

We are moving to a new town where we don't know anyone.

The future is very scary—if we think it is out of our control. And guess what—it is.

But the good news is that God is in control of your life today and will be tomorrow and the day after and the day after that. Yet, because we can't see maps of our lives, we get scared. We can't wait for God's time—we need to know *now*.

Jesus is fully God, but He also came to our world as a total human being. He understands the cares and loads we deal with. Yet He told us not to get ahead of ourselves.

Give your entire attention to what God is doing right now, and don't get worked up about what may or may not happen tomorrow. God will help you deal with whatever hard things come up when the time comes.

Get Ready for Eternity—You're Going to Spend a Lot of Time There

(Focusing on the Eternal)

A mother tried to deal with the trauma of the family cat's death by telling her young daughter, "Sammy is in heaven now." The little girl gave her mother a strange look then asked, "Why would God want a dead cat?"[1]

There are a lot of things about life—including death—that many folks just don't understand. And the tougher the times, the more people think about what's coming next. What about the afterlife? Is this all there is?

The fact is, God doesn't have much need for expired felines. But He does want us to know that this life isn't the end. It's only the beginning. Jesus said, "Do not let your hearts be troubled. Trust in God; trust also in me. In my Father's house are many rooms; if it were not so, I would have told you. I am going there to prepare a place for you. And if I go and prepare a place for you, I will come back and take you to be with me that you also may be where I am" (John 14:1-3). What did He promise? A philosophy? No. A pipe dream? No. A slice of pie in the sky? No.

He's gone to prepare a place—a dwelling place, an eternal place somewhere beyond the farthest star. When it's over here, it's just beginning over there. There really is life after life.

Now a man came up to Jesus and asked, "Teacher, what good thing must I do to get eternal life?"

"Why do you ask me about what is good?" Jesus replied. "There is only One who is good. If you want to enter life, obey the commandments."

"Which ones?" the man inquired.

Jesus replied, "'Do not murder, do not commit adultery, do not steal, do not give false testimony, honor your father and mother,' and 'love your neighbor as yourself.'"

"All these I have kept," the young man said. "What do I still lack?"

Jesus answered, "If you want to be perfect, go, sell your possessions and give to the poor, and you will have treasure in heaven. Then come, follow me."

When the young man heard this, he went away sad, because he had great wealth.

Then Jesus said to his disciples, "I tell you the truth, it is hard for a rich man to enter the kingdom of heaven. Again I tell you, it is easier for a camel to go through the eye of a needle than for a rich man to enter the kingdom of God."

When the disciples heard this, they were greatly astonished and asked, "Who then can be saved?"

Jesus looked at them and said, "With man this is impossible, but with God all things are possible" *(Matt. 19:16-26).*

Why did Jesus talk so much about eternal life?

Because He wasn't planted permanently in any earthly time zone. He was on His Heavenly Father's time—God's eternal time. I know that doesn't always compute. Most of us just can't comprehend infinity—even though its possibility is etched into the body of our Kodak cameras. (Remember that little overlapping "00" setting on your zoom lens?)

What's that double-0 life like? Well, for one thing, it's "out of this world."

Right away when you talk about life after death, someone with a Christian perspective thinks about heaven. But obviously not everyone thinks about it. Although 71 percent of Americans believe in an afterlife, we hear very little discussion about heaven in public or private. Philip Yancey commented on that strange fact writing in *Christianity Today.* He noted, "Percentages don't apply to eternity . . . but for the sake of argument, assume that ninety-nine percent of our existence will take place in heaven. Isn't it a little bizarre that we simply ignore heaven, acting as if it doesn't matter?"[2]

It is odd. We're surrounded by talk of the afterlife in various forms—reincarnation, out-of-body experiences, even ghosts—but you see few books or magazines devoted to the subject of heaven.

There could be many reasons for that. We're quite content here on earth, after all. Many people may be so comfortable here that they see no need to move on.

But move on we must. The Bible says, "It is appointed unto men once to die" (Heb. 9:27, KJV). That's an appointment you can't put in your daily planner. But you can be sure it's coming. We have an appointment with the afterlife—one day we'll pack up the things of time and move to eternity.

And that perspective of eternity (God's time zone) affects the way we think about living on earth. Jesus encountered a man who had some questions both about "moving on" and about living on earth. Nameless in this Gospel account, he was a ruler—probably a member of the ruling council, the religious-political bureaucracy of his day.

He acknowledged some spiritual questions and sought answers in a meeting with Jesus.

Right Search, Wrong Slant

The rich young man was on the right path—he was searching in the right direction. The global positioning system of his heart drew him to the right source: Jesus. And he was right about that. There are some answers that only He can provide.

But he had the wrong slant on the question. "What good things must I *do* to get eternal life?" Even though he was asking questions, he obviously thought he had all the answers. He thought there was something he could do to *earn* a spot in a promised and pleasant afterlife. After all, he had some frequent flyer miles left over.

The first thing we need to understand about eternal life is that it isn't earned. We can't buy *forever*. It comes as a bonus when we put our spiritual trust in the Lord Jesus Christ.

Let me illustrate. Doris Seger headed for her church office, intent on carving out a little practice time for her violin performance at that evening's service. But, upon entering her office, she was stunned to discover her beloved violin shattered all over the floor. Doris cherished that violin, an extravagant gift from her parents for high school graduation. She knew that they had scrimped and saved to buy her the beautiful instrument, and their sacrifice made it all the more valuable to her. Now, pieces of the wonderful violin littered her office. She wept at the sight.

A week after the incident, the police fingered the culprit, an 11-year-old boy named Eric who lived in the neighborhood. Doris went to visit Eric and his parents. The whole family seemed repentant for the boy's act, especially when Doris explained the significance of the violin. But before she left, Doris made sure to tell Eric that she forgave him for his act and that God would also offer forgiveness if Eric would ask.

A few days later, Doris's pastor received an unexpected visitor. Eric came to the church and asked if there were any odd jobs he might do to earn money for a new violin. The pastor, knowing Eric's true need, told him about the debt that has already been paid for all of us through the death of Jesus Christ. After their talk, Eric bowed his head and prayed to commit his life to Christ. One valuable instrument lost, one priceless soul gained. Doris Seger couldn't be happier with the trade.[3]

It's the same with eternal life. No amount of work can earn it. The rich young ruler soon found that out.

Who Set This Bar? And Why Is It So High?

Jesus told the ruler that the standard for self-induction into heaven's hall of fame was pretty high. "If you want to enter life, obey the commandments."

"Which ones?" the ruler quickly responded, as he wiped his brow in relief. He knew he could keep a couple of them with no sweat. After all, he was a college grad. He had worked his way up the corporate ladder and across the roof of the political house. This just might be a piece of cake.

But in Matthew 19 Jesus kept raising the bar. "Do not murder, do not commit adultery, do not steal, etc." The ruler thought there was still an outside chance (v. 20), "All these I have kept . . . What do I still lack?" After all, he was a charter member of the synagogue. He taught the newcomers class—and he got the job because he was squeaky clean (obviously not because he knew a lot about the Scriptures).

THINGS THAT GO BOOM IN THE NIGHT

His spiritual light was about to get a little dimmer. And he was about to get a nasty spiritual bump on his head. "Go, sell your possessions and give it to the poor, and you will have treasure in heaven . . . then come, follow me" (v. 21).

Boom! The ruler got hit with the bar that Jesus had raised! The eternal life that He promised wasn't based on either his net worth or his self-worth. It came as a result of a commitment to Christ. He was going to have to set his clock to GST—God's Supernatural Time, eternal time.

THE BEST STOCK OPTION AND THE WORLD'S WORST TRANSACTIONS

This ruler wasn't a Wall Street wonder! He had an opportunity to trade his stock in *time* for the unlimited wealth of *eternity*. But he refused the option. Instead he doubled his investment in the immediate—and only had a short-term gain. "When the young man heard this, he went away sad, because he had great wealth" (v. 22). He walked away from the greatest stock option ever offered: eternal life.

Eternal life is more than real estate; it's more than a mansion in heaven. (Though that is a promise as solid as granite. Remember, Jesus did promise us a dwelling place.)

Eternal life is a forever thing. It's an eternal reward—an existence and enjoyment beyond the boundaries of time.

Forever peace. Forever joy. Forever presence of the Lord. Forever reunion with believer friends and loved ones. Forever absence of sin and suffering. Forever day without night. Forever song without sorrow. Forever smiles without tears.

The ruler traded all of that for a percentage blip in his savings account, a chance that his mutual funds would gain a few points, the tenuous security of his 401(k), and a corner office in the state capitol.

"AND NOW, THE REST OF THE STORY"

What happened to the ruler after that sad talk? I don't know. The Bible doesn't say. But one thing I do know: Jesus didn't take him off heaven's mailing list. The stock options would be offered again. How do I know? In the words of the little Sunday School chorus, I know because "The Bible Tells Me So." His Word promises His constant invitation to enjoy the benefits of eternal life. "The Lord is not slow in keeping his promise, as some understand slowness. He is patient with you, not wanting anyone to perish, but everyone to come to repentance" (2 Pet. 3:9).

Hopefully, the rich young man didn't miss the next opportunity.

THE OPPORTUNITY OF AN ETERNAL LIFETIME!

You've heard about an opportunity of a lifetime. But how about the opportunity of an eternal lifetime? Given the opportunity, how much would you pay for a place in heaven? A recent survey asked that question to the wealthiest 1 percent of Americans. This elite group of about 1 million households earns at least $250,000 per year and has a net worth of at least $2.5 million. These millionaires gave the following breakdown of what they would spend on certain unique opportunities. For great beauty the average price they would willingly spend was $83,000. For talent they would spend $285,000. Great intellect commandeered $407,000. They said true love was worth $487,000.

The highest bid on any subject went for a place in heaven. To secure their spot in eternity, these wealthy Americans said they would part with $640,000. Isn't it interesting that even if heaven could be bought, those who have the most money don't want to spend more than 25 percent of their net worth to get there? What a stark contrast to the 100 percent investment Christ made to secure our eternal destiny.[4]

Like those polled, the rich young ruler was more concerned about his *wealth* than his *welfare*. I'm afraid the rich young man would have been right at home in the 21st century. Like many, he was conditioned to attach undue importance to the things of earth—the physical. He came to Jesus acknowledging Him as a teacher, come from God. He had heard about the results of His miracles, and maybe had seen a few of them himself. He understood religion and politics, but he didn't really know God.

How much like the young man are we? We try to measure spiritual things by physical yardsticks. For example, we evaluate the success of a church program by standards of the business world. We sometimes interpret Scripture in such a stereotypical manner that we squeeze every drop of life from a passage.

We focus on time instead of eternity. We're locked in the *now* instead of thinking about *then*.

The rich young man was sincere, at least, about discovering ultimate reality. But *seeking* truth is not the same as *accepting* it.

Aaron Burr was one of the greatest men in American history, and at the same time one of the most ignoble. His name lives in infamy as a traitor to our land. He died in disgrace and dishonor.

The turning point in his life came when he was a student at Princeton University. It was during a religious emphasis week that a speaker challenged every person to give his life to Christ. Aaron Burr stayed up late that night, pacing his room. He faced the ultimate question: Should I give my life to Jesus Christ or not? In the early morning hours he made his decision. Suddenly, he flung open the shutters of his dormitory and called out into the darkness: "Good-bye, Jesus Christ!" And he slammed the shutters shut.[5]

Finding Jesus is only the first step in gaining eternal life. You must also accept Him. It's amazing that some simply turn down His offer of forgiveness and the hope of eternal life. John 1:11-13, "He came to that which was his own, but his own did not receive him. Yet to all who received him, to those who believed in his name, he gave the right to become children of God—children born not of natural descent, nor of human decision or a husband's will, but born of God."

TWO BIRTHDAYS?

Awhile back I attended the birthday party for a 50-year-old. I attended it with a bit of uneasiness because I never figured the honoree would be that old so soon.

That birthday party was mine. (I particularly enjoyed the prune casserole and the Geritol milkshake.)

111

It was a milestone birthday, but it wasn't the most important. Many years before that, I invited the Lord Jesus Christ into my life. And by faith in Him, I became His child. I had a spiritual birthday. John Wesley said, "Faith is the condition and the only condition of salvation."

By faith alone, I was spiritually born into His family. My first birthday brought me physical life—but it was life that was limited by time. The psalmist in the Old Testament put a Spirit-powered calculator to it and came up with 70 years. "The length of our days is seventy years—or eighty, if we have the strength" (Ps. 90:10). That "if we have the strength" is gradually getting to be my life verse.

"Seventy years or eighty." Now I know that pills, Pepto-Bismol, and peroxide can push the margins a little, but the truth is, life on planet earth is limited. Our first birthday doesn't come with a lot of promises.

The second one is different. When we are born again into God's family, we have the promise of eternal living. That's a promise as familiar as that first Bible verse you learned in Sunday School, "For God so loved the world, that he gave his only begotten Son, that whosoever believeth in him should not perish, but have everlasting life" (John 3:16, KJV).

BIRTH IS AN IMPORTANT PART OF LIFE

That second birth isn't something that should be put off. According to new data from the Barna Research Group, surveys have determined the probability of people accepting Christ as their Savior in relation to a person's age. The data show that if a person does not accept Jesus Christ as Savior before the age of 14, the likelihood of ever doing so is slim.

Based on a nationwide representative sampling of more than 4,200 young people and adults, the survey data show that people from ages 5 through 13 have a 32 percent probability of accepting Christ as Savior. Young people from the ages of 14 through 18 have just a 4 percent likelihood of doing so, while adults (ages 19 through death) have only a 6 percent probability of making that choice.

This is H. A. Ironside's account of D. L. Moody's demonstration of how most people receive Christ when they are young:

When I was only twelve I went into an auditorium in Los Angeles. About 10,000 people were gathered in the building which had two galleries, a building that has since been torn down to make way for another. I went to hear D. L. Moody preach. Because I could find no other place, I crawled out on a rafter beneath the ceiling. There was Moody, giving his message. I remember how in the course of his address he said, "I want everyone in this auditorium who is a Christian, who knows he is a Christian, to stand up. Now, remain standing until the ushers can tell me about how many are on their feet." Then he said, "There are between 5,000 and 6,000 people standing. What a testimony—5,000 to 6,000 Christian people in this building! Now," he said, "I want everyone here who became a Christian before he was fifteen to sit down," and over half of that company sat down. Then he said, "Now how many of those who remain standing accepted Christ before they were twenty?" More than half of those remaining sat down. And then he went on, moving up the years by tens. "All who were saved before they were thirty, be seated," and a number sat down. "All who were saved before they were forty, be seated," and a smaller number sat down. And when he got to fifty, there were only about twenty left standing in that great congregation who had trusted Christ after they were fifty years of age! It was an object lesson I have never forgotten."[6]

This information is consistent with other studies that have shown that a large majority of Christians accept Jesus Christ as their Savior before they reach the age of 18. But this is the first study that has calculated people's probability of accepting Christ at different life stages. The data also challenge the widely held belief that the teenage years are prime years for evangelistic activity. Did you know that many well-known believers have been born again into God's family during their childhood? Rob Morgan gives us some vivid examples.

Polycarp, church father, was 9.

Matthew Henry, Bible commentator, was 11.

Jonathan Edwards, colonial evangelist, was 7.

E. Stanley Jones, missionary statesman, was 8 years old.

Corrie ten Boom, the *Tramp for the Lord* author, asked Christ to be her Savior at age 5.

W. A. Criswell, the famous Southern Baptist pastor, was saved when he was 10.

Philip Bliss, the hymn writer, was 12 years old.

William Booth, founder of the Salvation Army, was 15.

Count Nicholas Ludwig Zinzendorf, who gave rise to modern Protestant missions, was saved at age 4.

In the book *Zinger*, Ken Abraham, writing with golfer Paul Azinger, told about Azinger's use of a profound illustration during the sharing of his testimony about Christ. The professional golfer who has battled back onto the PGA after a life-threatening bout with cancer, told about a friend's unusual ride with a wealthy man on his private airplane. Next to Paul Azinger's friend sat a man with some very surprising surroundings. His seat was made of beautifully fashioned leather, a fan hung over his head, his tray-table was crafted from mahogany wood, and he was in arm's reach of a VCR, television, CD player, and his own computer.

Azinger's friend felt compelled to ask the obvious, "Why would anyone go to the expense to have all these things installed in an airplane?" The wealthy traveler replied, "Because this is my home." Azinger used this story to point out the tragedy of converting something into a home that was designed only for travel. This life is only for travel—taking us one day to our eternal home.[7]

Cartoonist Johnny Hart scripted a sobering reminder in a recent layout of his *Wizard of Id*. Hart, who also draws *B.C.*, frequently includes his Christian perspective on the pages of his artwork. In this particular strip he had one of the characters call into question an obituary that ended with "to be continued." How true. Death is by no means the end because every life will be continued in eternity. Make certain your continuation will be with Jesus Christ.[8]

American Express and the FBI aren't alone in granting rewards. God started it. His promise of life *after* death is a great incentive for life *before* death. In my book *The Buzzards Are Circling, but God's Not Finished with Me Yet*, I told a story that bears repeating here.

A while back, an old friend, Glen Payne, of the Cathedral Quartet fame, passed away. Gospel singer Mark Lowry sent the following e-mail to me while Jim Hill, the author of *What a Day That Will Be*, was in Oklahoma City singing for my church.

✝ 115

It's now Sunday night. I just got back from the funeral home. I saw Van, Glen's wife, and their children and their children's spouses. Van told me how Glen left this life. He would come in and out of consciousness and look wide-eyed toward the ceiling and around the room as if he was looking into eternity.

Over and over again, Glen would say "Wow!" as he viewed the other side. But when he finally passed away he was singing. Glen always said he wanted to go out of this life singing! Well he did! He was singing, *What a Day That Will Be*. When he came to the words, ". . . When He takes me by the hand . . ." Glen took his last breath on this earth.[9]

There'll be no sorrow there, no more burdens to bear,

No more sickness, no pain, no more parting over there.

And forever I will be with the One who died for me.

What a day, glorious day that will be!

What a day that will be when my Jesus I shall see,

And I look upon His face—the One who saved me by His grace.

When He takes me by the hand and leads me thro' the promised land,

What a day, glorious day that will be.[10]

What's on the other side? I don't know. I haven't been there yet. But I know if God planned it, it will beat anything Bob Vila ever imagined.

I also know that its quality as well as its quantity can begin in your life right now. You can have the assurance of life beyond the cemetery. You can experience an inner peace—a spiritual satisfaction right now.

Getting a good grip on life begins with getting a good focus on eternity. Thinking about what's to come will give you a better feeling about what you're going through now. Plan for it by surrendering your life to Christ. Let its promise fill your heart and your mind. Let its hope be the motivation for dwelling on the promises instead of the problems.

1. *Positive Living*, March/April 1997, 8.

2. Philip Yancey, "Heaven Can't Wait," *Christianity Today*, September 7, 1984, 53.

3. Doris Louise Seger, "Shattered!" *Herald of Holiness*, April 1997, 18-19.

4. *HomeLife*, July 1998, 66.

5. Dr. Robert H. Schuller, *Reach Out for New Life* (Garden Grove, Calif.: Cathedral Press, 1977 and 1991), 699.

6. H. A. Ironside, *Lectures on the Book of Acts* (Neptune, N.J.: Loizeaux, 1943), 586-87.

7. Paul Azinger with Ken Abraham, *Zinger* (Grand Rapids: Zondervan Publishing House, 1995), 250-51.

8. *Wizard of Id*, 10/9/97.

9. Stan Toler, *The Buzzards May Be Circlin', but God's Not Finished with Me Yet*, (Tulsa, Okla.: Honor Books, 2001), 124.

10. Jim Hill, *What a Day That Will Be*. Copyright 1955 by Ben L. Speer (SESAC), Ben Speer Music, P.O. Box 40201, Nashville, TN 37204.

When You Get to the End
of Your Rope, There's Hope
(Understanding God's Forgiveness)

A heavily booked commercial flight out of Baltimore, Maryland, was canceled, and a single agent was re-booking a long line of inconvenienced travelers. Suddenly an angry passenger pushed his way to the front and slapped his ticket down on the counter. "I have to be on this flight and it has to be first class!" he insisted.

"I'm sorry, sir," the agent replied. "I'll be happy to help you, but I have to take care of these folks first."

The passenger was unimpressed. "Do you have any idea who I am?" he demanded in a voice loud enough for the passengers behind him to hear.

Without hesitating, the gate agent smiled and picked up her public-address microphone. "May I have your attention, please?" she broadcast throughout the terminal. "We have a passenger here at the gate who does not know who he is. If anyone can help him find his identity, please come to the gate."

As the man retreated, the people in the terminal burst into applause.

Jesus went to the Mount of Olives. At dawn he appeared again in the temple courts, where all the people gathered around him, and he sat down to teach them. The teachers of the law and the Pharisees brought in a woman caught in adultery. They made her stand before the group and said to Jesus, "Teacher, this woman was caught in the act of adultery. In the Law Moses commanded us to stone such women. Now what do you say?" They were using this question as a trap, in order to have a basis for accusing him.

But Jesus bent down and started to write on the ground with his finger. When they kept on questioning him, he straightened up and said to them, "If any one of you is without sin, let him be the first to throw a stone at her." Again he stooped down and wrote on the ground.

At this, those who heard began to go away one at a time, the older ones first, until only Jesus was left, with the woman still standing there. Jesus straightened up and asked her, "Woman, where are they? Has no one condemned you?"

"No one, sir," she said.

"Then neither do I condemn you," Jesus declared. "Go now and leave your life of sin."

When Jesus spoke again to the people, he said, "I am the light of the world. Whoever follows me will never walk in darkness, but will have the light of life" *(John 8:1-12)*.

"Jesus Christ stands alone in history, in teaching, in example, in character, an exception, a marvel, and He is himself the evidence of Christianity" (A. T. Pierson).

Marjorie Holmes was struggling with some past failures in her life when she got an interesting letter from a friend. The stationery recounted a recent visit this woman had with her granddaughter when they got to see a plane write messages in the sky. The young girl loved watching the words being drawn in the air but was puzzled when the letters started disappearing. She studied the situation for a moment then suddenly blurted out, "Maybe Jesus has an eraser!"[1]

Maybe you need an eraser. Maybe the burden of one or more incidents in your past has sucked the joy out of your life. Maybe you're at the end of your rope—you've tried everything you know to find relief for that inner aching of your heart.

If that's the case, then I have some great news: *God's at the end of your rope.* There is forgiveness there. There is contentment there. There is purpose there.

Heaven waits to heal your horror. A faceless, nameless woman in the Bible found that out. She had a past the size of two aircraft carriers. And the burden she felt was exceeded only by the burden others wished to place upon her.

But then she met the Burden-bearer. She met Jesus, and in one glorious moment in time, she found deliverance.

Let's take a heartfelt look at this wonderful story.

THE AWKWARD ACCUSATION

"The teachers of the law and the Pharisees brought in a woman caught in adultery. They made her stand before the group and said to Jesus, 'Teacher, this woman was caught in the act of adultery'" (vv. 3-4).

She was *caught on tape* as they would say in TV land. Her private sin was suddenly publicly exposed. She couldn't deny it.

121

Someone from the "Jerusalem's Most Wanted" staff had followed the grimy trail of her immoral lifestyle and reported her activities to the religious authorities.

These crusty custodians of public morality, religious zealots called Pharisees, angrily took over. They dragged her, shamed and distraught, to the streets and pointed a mocking and accusing finger.

What upstanding citizens. They were clearing the streets of the riffraff.

Let's be clear about this. This "religious" bunch wasn't there to sweep the streets. They were there to exalt themselves and to make a public spectacle of someone's sin. They had no interest in a fair hearing. They had one purpose in mind: to condemn her—and to trap Jesus in the process, if at all possible. They came to "judge" and "jury" the woman, in hopes of wiping out an opposing philosophy—one whose core value was compassion and mercy.

But the woman's sexual sin wasn't the only thing on display that day. The tyranny and hypocrisy of the Pharisees were also being exposed. Where was her partner in sin? Adultery involves two people. Where was the man? Why wasn't he brought before Jesus for the same public humiliation? Unfortunately, the kind of shame that this woman experienced is not uncommon in many cultures. It's almost a paragraph from one of our current news articles.

Religion isn't a very good cover-up. We can attend three services a week, bow five times a day, or recite certain prayers until we're hoarse, and still have enough evil stuff in our hearts to gag a hyena.

It's no use trying to bury a past in some pious activity. The piety will eventually turn to panic. Let me illustrate. While fishing offshore in his small boat, a man fell overboard and immediately started to panic. Since he was alone, he quickly turned to God. He cried out, "Lord, please save me! If You'll just let me live I'll start keeping the Ten Commandments. Thou shalt not . . . uh . . . Thou shalt not . . . uh . . ." Frustrated, the man suddenly cried out, "Oh God, if You'll just get me out of this I promise to *learn* the Ten Commandments."[2]

Somebody will eventually find out how little piety is left. And the hurt that goes along with the revelation will probably seem unbearable.

Maybe you've been accused. Maybe something you buried in the attic of your life has suddenly been dragged into the streets. Maybe you've tried to use "religion" as a cover. But it didn't work, and you're at the end of your rope.

Guess what? There's hope.

Read on.

The Law and Order

The Pharisees continued their kangaroo court: "'In the Law Moses commanded us to stone such women. Now what do you say?' They were using this question as a trap, in order to have a basis for accusing him" (vv. 5-6).

What could He say? Jesus hadn't come to earth to abolish the law of God. He hadn't come to amend the Ten Commandments. He wasn't going to add one or drop another simply because it didn't fit the times or because it made someone as uncomfortable as a dachshund in a Great Dane show! Jesus was clear about that. "Do not think that I have come to abolish the Law or the Prophets; I have not come to abolish them but to fulfill them" (Matt. 5:17).

123

God's standards aren't given to make us *squirm*. He has given them to make us *firm*—to make us solid in character and confident in our conduct.

> Teach me knowledge and good judgment, for I believe in your commands. Before I was afflicted I went astray, but now I obey your word. You are good, and what you do is good; teach me your decrees. Though the arrogant have smeared me with lies, I keep your precepts with all my heart. Their hearts are callous and unfeeling, but I delight in your law *(Ps. 119:66-70)*.

God's law and order is for our protection. We can delight in it. It is the source of our peace—not panic.

But maybe someone has tried to trap you in the law. Maybe someone has tried to *add* to the law by imposing his or her own version of its standards.

Maybe it goes back farther than your first driving test. (The Lord knows how judgmental a driving instructor can be!) Maybe it goes all the way back to the dinner table of your childhood. Maybe over a bowl of chicken soup someone tried to force you into a mold by equating your goodness with the way you held your soup spoon. Now I know that's on the fringe—but you know what I mean. Maybe you're at the end of your rope, trying to keep laws that God hasn't given in the first place. That's pretty heavy baggage.

Joan Borysenko wrote about the man who went to the luggage store to buy a new suitcase for his guilt. The old one was full. The man found just the ticket, a marvelous item designed by a panel of psychiatrists and leather craftsmen. It had compartments for every kind of guilt imaginable, including guilt for working too hard and guilt for goofing off, guilt for not making enough money and guilt for making too much, guilt for successful ventures and guilt for failure. And there was plenty of room for miscellaneous guilt. It even had wheels for dragging it through the airport.[3]

Are you carrying baggage? If so, there's hope at the end of your rope.

Notice Jesus' next move.

THE DEAFENING DEFENSE

"Jesus bent down and started to write on the ground with his finger. When they kept on questioning him, he straightened up and said to them, 'If any one of you is without sin, let him be the first to throw a stone at her'" (vv. 6-7). Suddenly you could hear the silence—louder than a 200-watt woofer in the backseat of a Toyota.

Whatever He wrote on the ground couldn't compare with the look in His eyes when He stood up. He looked past the accusations into the hearts of the accusers.

"Let's talk about law, fellas. Anybody here ever look on a woman with adultery in your heart?"

Silence.

"Anybody here ever tell a lie?"

"Anybody here ever get so angry with someone they wished they were dead?"

Probably the Pharisees started to feel a little faint at this point—because they got the point. There isn't a sliding scale of sin. Disobedience against the will and word of God has a *spirit* of rebellion as well as an *act* of rebellion.

The defense was deafening.

But it didn't excuse the adulterous woman. It simply exposed the judgmental and sinful attitude of her accusers.

✝ 125

The fact is, Jesus can never excuse sin—of any kind. But another fact is equally important. Though Jesus can never excuse sin, He can never *refuse* the sinner. "Whoever comes to me I will never drive away" (John 6:37).

Maybe no one has come to your defense. Maybe you feel as alone as any human being could ever feel. Here's the good news: When everyone has left you, Jesus will stand by you—never late, never accusing—but always on time, and always wanting to forgive. It's the next verse—you know, the one right after John 3:16: "For God did not send his Son into the world to condemn the world, but to save the world through him" (v. 17).

Richard Bolles, who has influenced many people through the ministry of his best-selling book *What Color Is Your Parachute?* preached a sermon for the installation of a pastor in which he made the following comments: "We are a people whose weaknesses are part of God's plan. God neither creates that weakness, nor ordains it, but He does have a plan for how to deal with it when it inevitably appears. The plan is forgiveness."

When you've come to the end of your rope—there's hope. The adulterous woman discovered it.

THE SAVIOR'S SUPREME COURT

"At this, those who heard began to go away one at a time, the older ones first, until only Jesus was left, with the woman still standing there" (v. 9). One by one, the accusers stepped backward, slinking from the sight of the Galilean. It was too much for them to bear. Suddenly, their shame *out-shamed* the very woman they had dragged before the courts of earth.

Now she was alone—alone before the One at whose knee eventually the whole world will bow. Alone before the One whose life would be the final standard of right living.

126

Alone before heaven's Chief Justice—"with the woman still standing there."

How would you feel? A bit nervous? Probably.

But she was relieved to be standing there alone. Now she wouldn't have to answer to anyone but Jesus. Everyone else had packed up their evidence in their blue, see-through Tupperware boxes and headed back to the office.

Charlotte Elliot came to Caesar Milan and asked how she could become a Christian. The old man replied, "My dear, it is very simple. You have only to come to Jesus."

And she said to him, "But I am a very great sinner. Will He take me just as I am?"

"Yes, He will take you just as you are, and no other way."

And then she said, "If He will take me just as I am, then I will come," and she went home to her room, sat down at her desk, and wrote the beautiful words of the gospel song.

Just as I am without one plea,

O Lamb of God, I come, I come.

And aren't you glad you only have to answer to Him? Aren't you glad He will hear your final appeal? Aren't you glad the verdict will come from the heart of a Savior who loved the world so much that He offered His life's blood to bear its guilt?

THE VICTORIOUS VERDICT

Now Jesus turned to the woman. Maybe His hand lifted her chin. Maybe He stood at a distance in silence, waiting for her curiosity to take over and for her to lift her face to look into His eyes.

What a moment.

127

The verdict was in. Her heart knew the words she needed to hear. And she knew full well that only Jesus could say them—only He could offer a verdict over her life. She was at the end of her rope, and time was running out.

Jesus straightened up and asked her, "Woman, where are they? Has no one condemned you?"

"No one, sir," she said.

"Then neither do I condemn you," Jesus declared. "Go now and leave your life of sin" (vv. 10-11).

The verdict: freedom. The victorious verdict.

I don't know all of the conversation that transpired in those moments. I do know that the only thing Jesus can do with sin is to forgive it. He can't excuse it. And we can't hide it. We only find His forgiveness when we 'fess up. The scripture is clear: "Repent and be baptized, every one of you, in the name of Jesus Christ for the forgiveness of your sins. And you will receive the gift of the Holy Spirit" (Acts 2:38). *Repent* means to agree with God that our disobedience against Him is sin—and to agree to stop sinning.

I've experienced His great healing forgiveness personally. I wrote about it in my book *God Has Never Failed Me, but He's Sure Scared Me to Death a Few Times.* Several years ago, I attended a service where my friend, Dr. H. B. London Jr., now assistant to the president of Focus on the Family, was preaching. As we entered the sanctuary, each attendee received a brown paper lunch bag that was labeled "God Bag." In addition, white strips of paper were distributed to each person. As Dr. London concluded his powerful message, he asked each person in attendance to write down his or her hurts, problems, and needs and put them in the God Bag. I joined with others in making my list.

One hurt was especially painful to write down. A person whom I had employed and had trusted as a friend had betrayed me. It appeared that the lie that was being told about me would never be corrected. Because it raised questions about my integrity, I was especially hurt and upset. Day after day, I had thought about the incident, often weeping bitterly in prayer, asking God to deal with my offender.

Finally, after allowing each of us time to finish writing, Dr. London instructed each person to prayerfully commit their concerns to the Lord and put them into the bag. And he told us to remove the strips of paper only as our prayers were answered.

With a sense of relief and childlike faith, I placed my concerns into the God Bag. I felt better immediately! (Yes, even about my offender.)

Daily I began praying the Lord's Prayer. In that prayer, Jesus taught us to pray, "Forgive us our debts as we forgive our debtors." I chose not to curse or rehearse my hurts. I cupped my hands before the Lord and symbolically gave them over to God. I then raised my hands in prayer (both hands—pretty good for a Nazarene) and claimed victory over my hurts.

Time passed and with each answer to prayer, I removed a strip of paper and gave thanks to God. Five years passed, and all but one strip of paper had been removed. You guessed it—there had been no contact from my offender. Then, one Saturday evening as I sat putting the finishing touches on my Sunday morning message titled "What Is Forgiveness?" the phone rang. It was the person who had attacked my credibility.

The tearful voice said, "It's been years since I've talked to you. Will you forgive me for lying about you? Christ has forgiven me, and now I need to know—Stan, will you forgive me?" Without hesitation, I said, "You have my forgiveness!"

What peace flooded my soul as I went to my office and took out the last strip of paper from the God Bag! God is never late in matters of forgiveness. He knows the very moment that our souls need relief![4]

The woman caught in adultery found hope at the end of her rope. Her failure was turned to forgiveness, her sadness to salvation—because her sorrow was turned to surrender.

She surrendered her past to the God at the end of her rope. And discovered a glorious future.

What was next for her? "Go now and leave your life of sin."

While swimming at the beach, a young boy got caught in the undertow and began crying out for help. With no lifeguard on duty, an avid swimmer quickly swam to his rescue. When they fell to the sand after surviving the pull of that current, the boy exclaimed, "Thank you, sir, for saving my life!"

The man waited to catch his breath, then looked straight into the boy's eyes. He gave a slight smile and then said, "Just do me one favor. Make sure your life was worth saving."[5]

---

1. *Today's Christian Woman,* July/August 1992, 19.

2. *Beaumont Examiner,* 7/8/99, 17.

3. Joan Borysenko, *Guilt Is the Teacher, Love Is the Lesson* (New York: Warner Books, Inc., 1990), 26.

4. Stan Toler, *God Has Never Failed Me, but He's Sure Scared Me to Death a Few Times* (Tulsa, Okla.: Honor Books, 2001), 137-38.

5. *A Second Helping of Chicken Soup for the Soul* (Canfield & Hansen, 1995), 12.

Don't Grab the Steering Wheel While God's Driving
(Resting in God's Timing)

The new minister came to his office the first morning of his new assignment. He found three envelopes on his desk from the previous pastor.

The first was marked, "Open if you run into trouble."

On the second was the note, "Open if you run into bad trouble."

The third read, "Open if the trouble is disastrous."

There was no need to open any envelope for quite some time. But the honeymoon finally ended and the young pastor found he was having difficulty. He remembered the envelopes that he had put away in a drawer. He opened the first envelope and found this suggestion: "Blame your predecessor." He took the advice and it seemed to work—at least for a while.

Things went along fine for quite some time and then trouble, more serious this time, struck. It was time for the second

131

envelope, which he quickly opened. This time he read, "Blame the denomination." Again he found relief. He was grateful for the letters.

A few years later, trouble returned to his congregation, and this time, it was really bad. Once more, he sought guidance from the helpful words of his predecessor. He went to the drawer, opened the third envelope, and read, "Prepare three envelopes."

Maybe you're in the process of preparing some envelopes right now.

Wouldn't it be great if the answer to some of life's troubles was as simple as opening some "magic envelope"?

Some things in life not only leave us speechless but also leave us clueless.

Financial difficulties.

Broken relationships.

Sudden illness.

Job insecurity.

What do we do now? We're a little bit like Mike, a famous former resident of Fruita, Colorado. Fruita recently honored this distinguished citizen with a sculpture placed on a downtown corner. In March of 2000, sculptor Lyle Nichols unveiled the four-foot masterpiece titled Mike the Headless Chicken. It is a reminder of what happened in Fruita nearly 60 years earlier.

Back in the 1940s, farmer Lloyd Olsen prepared to lop off the head of one of his chickens, one he had named Mike. Wanting to preserve as much of the neck for dinner as possible, he laid his ax at the base of Mike's skull, raised the sharp blade, and WHOOSH! That's the end of ol' Mike, right?

Wrong.

Mike survived the attack and became a bizarre piece of history—a headless folk hero. Olsen not only didn't eat the bird but he actually started to care for it. Of course, headless Mike had to make some life adjustments. He went through the motions of pecking for the food but couldn't get anything. And when he tried to crow only a slight gurgle came out.

Farmer Olsen fed this strange chicken with an eyedropper, and after a week of survival, he took Mike to some scientists at the University of Utah. They theorized the chicken had enough brain stem left to live without his head.

Mike the Headless Chicken made it into *Life* magazine and the *Guinness Book of World Records*. He became quite an attraction until he choked to death on a kernel of corn in an Arizona motel eighteen months after surviving the chopping block.[1]

Maybe you're a survivor as well. Though I seriously doubt that you have been beheaded and lived to tell about it. Like Mike, you may be trying to maneuver through life without any real direction. Or worse yet, you may know about the direction that your Heavenly Father wants to give, and you keep grabbing the steering wheel away from Him! Maybe you think that by taking over you can get to where you want to go a bit faster.

What are you experiencing right now?

What is that situation that's trying your patience, stretching your endurance, or testing your courage?

Do you need to know the way? Are you confused, desperate?

Do you feel like time is running out?

Then it's time to hand the steering wheel over to God. It's time to rest in God's timely help in the face of your situation, the need of your heart, and the circumstances of your life.

Understand this: His help is never late, and seldom early; He's always right on time. The psalmist understood it. "The LORD is my strength and my shield; my heart trusts in him, and

I am helped. My heart leaps for joy and I will give thanks to him in song" (Ps. 28:7).

Joy-jumps during a rugged journey? A song in the storm? How on earth?

Let me give you some important principles—principles that helped me when it seemed like time was running out.

PRINCIPLE NUMBER 1: NO PROBLEM IS TOO BIG FOR GOD

When God led His people, Israel, He gave them some accompanying directions.

> Obey the LORD your God and keep his commands and decrees that are written in this Book of the Law and turn to the LORD your God with all your heart and with all your soul.
>
> Now what I am commanding you today is not too difficult for you or beyond your reach. It is not up in heaven, so that you have to ask, "Who will ascend into heaven to get it and proclaim it to us so we may obey it?" Nor is it beyond the sea, so that you have to ask, "Who will cross the sea to get it and proclaim it to us so we may obey it?" No, the word is very near you; it is in your mouth and in your heart so you may obey it *(Deut. 30:10-14).*

Did you get that? It's "not beyond your reach." What isn't? God's unlimited power.

No wonder J. I. Packer said, "Belief that divine guidance is real rests upon two foundation-facts: first, the reality of God's plan for us; second, the ability of God to communicate with us. On both these facts the Bible has much to say."

What's the biggest personal problem you can imagine? Divorce? Unemployment? Addiction? Abandonment? Abuse? The problems may be so great and have so many implications that they may seem insurmountable.

But the good news is that the "Word is near you." No problem is too big for God. Your reaching out in faith and obedience to His Word unlocks its promises.

"He who dwells in the shelter of the Most High will rest in the shadow of the Almighty. I will say of the LORD, 'He is my refuge and my fortress, my God, in whom I trust.' Surely he will save you from the fowler's snare and from the deadly pestilence. He will cover you with his feathers, and under his wings you will find refuge; his faithfulness will be your shield and rampart" (Ps. 91:1-4).

God can do anything, and I mean *anything!* If He parted the Red Sea, fed the 5,000, and raised the dead, He is more than able to handle the details (including the dangers) of your life.

Oddly, the reason that many people don't experience God's help is that they don't ask for it. Ken Blanchard, author of the best-seller *The One Minute Manager,* is now a Christian, but prior to his conversion he needed a powerful challenge from well-known pastor Bill Hybels to get him thinking seriously about Christ. Hybels knew that Blanchard carried a bedrock belief in the enormous value of utilizing business consultants. For this reason he gave Dr. Blanchard the following counsel. Pastor Hybels said, "You need to call in three consultants that could really help you . . . the Father, Son, and Holy Spirit." When we need guidance in any area of our lives we can't find a better group of consultants.

PRINCIPLE NUMBER 2: NO PERSON IS TOO INSIGNIFICANT FOR GOD'S HELP

I know what you're thinking. "If Billy Graham were in trouble, all of heaven would be on highest alert." You're right about that. Dr. Graham always had the right to call on heaven's forces in times of personal danger. But the fact is, you have the same access. "The LORD remembers us and will bless us: He will bless the house of Israel, he will bless the house of Aaron, he will bless those who fear the LORD—small and great alike" (Ps. 115:12-13).

Wow. "Small and great alike." If you're a child of God by faith in the Lord Jesus Christ, it really doesn't matter what side of the tracks you come from—religious or otherwise—your Heavenly Father is committed to your care. On His own schedule, in keeping with His perfect direction, and according to His unlimited power, He has promised to get you where you ought to go.

As surely as there is no problem too big for God to handle, there is no person too small for His attention. Remember Zacchaeus, the little man in the Bible who wanted to see Jesus? He was so anxious to meet the Lord that he went to Lowe's, bought the best ladder he could find with his Jericho Express Card, and climbed to the tallest limb of a tree just to get a look at Him (Luke 19). I've always been moved by that wonderful story. When I was a child in Sunday School, the familiar song about that "wee little man" drove home a wonderful truth to me: There is no size requirement in God's care plan.

Maybe you'd have to jump up to shake the hand of the fellow painted on that sign at the amusement park—you know the one that qualifies you to be tall enough to ride the roller coaster. You may feel insignificant on the inside, but you're big in God's eyes.

You could be kneeling down, tying the player's shoelaces in the middle of a New York Knicks basketball team huddle, but God can spot a frown on your face from the farthest outpost of heaven.

Maybe you're so young and inexperienced someone is reading this book to you. But you're still a candidate for God's care. Remember when the disciples tried to shoo children away from Jesus? The kids got a hug and the disciples got a lecture. Nobody's too small for God.

PRINCIPLE NUMBER 3: NO EARTHLY WISDOM IS GREATER THAN GOD'S

Where do you go for direction?

People look for answers in many places—and sometimes in all the wrong places. From the earthbound advice of unbelieving friends to the one-size-fits-all ramblings of late-night TV psychics, earth's counsel is limited at best and corrupt at worst. There is only one source of true wisdom: God.

"Blessed is the man who does not walk in the counsel of the wicked or stand in the way of sinners or sit in the seat of mockers. But his delight is in the law of the LORD, and on his law he meditates day and night" (Ps. 1:1-2).

A recent article titled "178 Seconds to Live" chronicled the results of an aviation study. Twenty pilots took their turn in a flight simulator. Each of the pilots was a skilled aviator, but none had any instrument training. As long as they could see where they were going—as long as the weather was good—they were all experts in flight. Then the pilots in the simulator were asked to keep their plane under control as they flew through rough weather. Everything changed when they could no longer fly by sight. All 20 of the pilots lost control of their planes in an average time span of just 178 seconds. In a real-life situation, the same pilots who were very capable of keeping a plane aloft in good weather wouldn't have survived *three minutes.*

137

But you and I aren't journeying through life in a simulator. When we hit bad weather, it's the real thing.

Most of us can handle life when the conditions are partly cloudy, but when the storms come we need much more than conventional wisdom and gut-level intuition. The good news is we don't have to! Whether the skies are bright and blue or the storm clouds are beginning to brew, we have a *flight manual* and a *map* rolled into one: God's Word. God has given us a fast-track course in instrument training—the wisdom of heaven is a page away. And the Holy Spirit applies the directions just when we need them.

Have you been in any storms lately? Are you trying to fly "visual" instead of "instrument"?

Don't.

Jesus knows the directions better than anyone. I heard a story that illustrates it. Once upon a time, there was a famous and very successful sea captain. For years, he guided merchant ships all over the world, and never once was bested by stormy seas or pirates. He was admired by his crew and fellow captains alike.

Every morning, he went through a strange ritual. He locked himself in his captain's quarters and opened a small safe. In the safe was an envelope with a piece of paper inside. He stared at the paper for a minute, then locked it back up and went about his daily duties.

For years this went on, and his crew became very curious. Was it a treasure map? A letter from a long-lost love? Everyone speculated about the contents of the envelope.

One day, the captain died. After burying his body at sea, the first mate led the entire crew into the captain's quarters, where he opened the safe, pulled out the envelope, opened the folded sheet of paper and read, PORT IS LEFT, STARBOARD IS RIGHT.

Do you have to look for a message in a locked safe to know which way to go?

What promise has God already given you? Will you believe it? What command has God already placed on you? Will you obey it? What truth has He already offered you? Will you accept it?

Faith is trusting God's wisdom and deliverance, even when all human hope is gone—even when we face *actual* weather conditions. "My soul faints with longing for your salvation, but I have put my hope in your word" (Ps. 119:81).

PRINCIPLE NUMBER 4: FASTING AND PRAYER LEAD TO VICTORY

Fasting is abstaining from something (anything from food to TV watching) for the purpose of spending that time in spiritual pursuits. Fasting is most often linked with prayer. Many of the major religions of the world practice fasting as a personal, spiritual discipline. Throughout the Bible, fasts were called to seek God's direction and blessing. Prayer and fasting is a way to spiritual victory.

King Jehoshaphat is a marvelous example.

Time was running out for Israel's King Jehoshaphat. The enemy was knocking on the door of his kingdom. A soldier brought him a bad-news message. But what Jehoshaphat did next made him a victor before the first arrow ever flew.

"Alarmed, Jehoshaphat resolved to inquire of the LORD, and he proclaimed a fast for all Judah. The people of Judah came together to seek help from the LORD; indeed, they came from every town in Judah to seek him" (2 Chron. 20:3-4).

While writing this book, I received word that Dr. Bill Bright, founder of Campus Crusade for Christ, had died. I quickly reflected on a conversation that I had with Dr. Bright a few months before. He told me he was in the midst of a "40-day Daniel fast." Considering he was desperately ill and had been told by the doctors that he had only a few months to live, I was speechless! This godly man testified that he had completed *twelve* 40-day fasts over the past eight years. I was greatly challenged by the fact that he had chosen this perilous time in his life to start another fast. But Dr. Bright had a burden for world revival, and he knew the secret of victory: Great things happen when we deny self and call on God in believing faith.

The timing was perfect.

This man of God was on God's time—and God's time isn't subject to the pains or problems of earth. It has eternity in view, even in the midst of earthly suffering.

Before James Garfield became president of the United States, he was principal of Hiram College in Ohio. A father once asked him if a particular course of study could be simplified so that his son could go through by a shorter route.

"Certainly," replied Garfield. "But it all depends upon what you want to make of your boy. When God wants to make an oak tree, he takes a hundred years. When he wants to make a squash, he requires only two summers."

"The plans of the LORD stand firm forever, the purposes of his heart through all generations" (Ps. 33:11).

PRINCIPLE NUMBER 5: GOD IS ALWAYS GOOD

The little prayer you learned as a child is right in both cases: *"God is great* and *God is good."*

You may not be confident of anything else, but you can be sure that God is good—even when bad things happen. "I am still confident of this: I will see the goodness of the LORD in the land of the living" (Ps. 27:13). Now that's a whole lot better than a testimonial for toothpaste! That's something you can chew on even when you don't have any teeth left.

Based on the authority of the Word of God, "you will see the goodness of the LORD in the land of the living." That's *real-time* living. God's time is full of His goodness.

It's everywhere. God is good to you in the hospital. God is good to you at the loan office. God is good to you at the automotive service center. His goodness flows unhindered by the bad stuff. There is no supply shortage when it comes to God's goodness.

Marilyn vos Savant is listed in *Guinness Book of World Records* for having the highest IQ. Her brilliant insight was reflected in a recent column where she humorously said, "The real wealth of this country is not stored in Fort Knox. It is in 'the back.'" She noted how often the item we want is not on the shelf but is found "in the back." How many times have you asked a store employee for an item, "Do you have any more in the back?" Sometimes we're pleasantly surprised when the salesperson returns from the back with our desired product. But many times we learn there aren't any in the back either.[2]

When the children of Israel were wandering in the desert they had a "senior moment." They answered their own silly question even before they asked it. "When he struck the rock, water gushed out, and streams flowed abundantly. But can he also give us food? Can he supply meat for his people?" (Ps. 78:20).

They forgot that God has an unlimited supply "in the back." Let's not be guilty of missing a $200 question on "Who

Wants to Be a Millionaire?" What we need may not be in plain sight, but God always has our needed provision in the back.

Sometimes that walk from "the back" seems to take a long time. Sometimes we have more month than money. Sometimes the demand seems greater than the supply. But that doesn't throw God's timing off. He'll seldom be early, but you can be sure He'll never be late. He'll always be on time.

PRINCIPLE NUMBER 6: LOOK AT THE *LORD* NOT THE *LOAD*

Let me ask you a rather personal question. Are you problem-focused or God-focused? If you're like most people, you tend to look more at your problems. But focusing on problems means putting them first—even in front of your faith. What a waste of a precious moment! It's like a shy date spending valuable time staring at the scuff of a shoe instead of gazing into the eyes of a beloved, and hearing words of affirmation and affection. Focus on God, not on your problem.

The apostle Paul gave some pretty good advice about focus. "Therefore we do not lose heart. Though outwardly we are wasting away, yet inwardly we are being renewed day by day. For our light and momentary troubles are achieving for us an eternal glory that far outweighs them all. So we fix our eyes not on what is seen, but on what is unseen. For what is seen is temporary, but what is unseen is eternal" (2 Cor. 4:16-18).

Focusing on the outward—the earthly, is like being on the devil's diet plan, you end up wasting away. Focusing on the promises and presence of an eternal God—the eternal, unseen—means we are gaining ground every day. It's better to be on God's time.

PRINCIPLE NUMBER 7: GOD HAS A PROMISE FOR EVERY
PROBLEM

Everest Storms was a schoolteacher in Kitchener, Ontario,
when he took the challenge to discover how many promises
were in the Bible. For a year and a half he scoured the pages of
Scripture and took detailed notes. During his 27th reading of
the entire Bible, Storms concluded that the Bible contains
7,487 promises by God to man. 2 Pet. 1:4 reminds us that
God's promises are "precious and magnificent," and Rom. 3:4
assures us that God can be trusted to deliver on His promises.[3]

God doesn't make promises like some corrupt councilman
with a tax fraud indictment hanging over his head. He makes
promises (and keeps them) from the very core of His being.

God's very character is at stake when He says He will do
something. A promissory note from God is worth infinitely
more than any silver certificate of earth.

What do you need? Provision, forgiveness, strength? You
got it.

The Old Testament leader Joshua had a pretty good handle
on that truth. It was one of the last things he said to his people—and we know how important last words are: "Now I am
about to go the way of all the earth. You know with all your
heart and soul that not one of all the good promises the LORD
your God gave you has failed. Every promise has been fulfilled;
not one has failed" (Josh. 23:14).

In 18th-century Wales, a young man named William
Williams graduated from the university as a physician but quickly changed professions to become a physician of the soul—a
clergyman.

During his 43 years of itinerant ministry, Williams traveled

143

more than 95,000 miles, and his impassioned preaching drew crowds of 10,000 or more. Once he spoke to an estimated crowd of 80,000, noting in his journal, "God strengthened me to speak so loud that most could hear."

William Williams is best remembered, however, for his hymns, becoming in Wales what Isaac Watts was in England. In all, he composed over 800 hymns, his best known being an autobiographical prayer. Williams had lived as a pilgrim, pressing on through the snow of winter, the rains of springtime, and the heat of fall. He was beaten by mobs (once within an inch of his life) and cheered by crowds, but in all his travels he sought only to do the will of God, saying:

> *Guide me, O Thou great Jehovah,*
> *Pilgrim through this barren land;*
> *I am weak, but Thou art mighty;*
> *Hold me with Thy powerful hand.*[4]

Knowing God's Word is a sure comfort when trouble comes. The more familiar you are with Scripture, the greater help it will become. But you need to have a greater understanding of the Bible than the young minister displayed as he interviewed for his first pastor job. The pulpit committee chairman asked, "Son, do you know the Bible pretty good?"

The young minister said, "Yes, pretty good."

The chairman asked, "Which part do you know best?"

He responded saying, "I know the New Testament best."

"Which part of the New Testament do you know best?" asked the chairman.

The young minister said, "Several parts."

The chairman said, "Well, why don't you tell us the story of the Prodigal Son."

The young man said, "Fine."

"There was a man of the Pharisees named Nicodemus, who went down to Jericho by night and he fell upon stony ground and the thorns choked him half to death.

"The next morning Solomon and his wife, Gomorrah, came by, and carried him down to the ark for Moses to take care of. But, as he was going through the Eastern Gate into the Ark, he caught his hair in a limb and he hung there forty days and forty nights and he afterwards did hunger. And the ravens came and fed him.

"The next day, the three wise men came and carried him down to the boat dock and he caught a ship to Nineveh. And when he got there he found Delilah sitting on the wall. He said, 'chunk her down, boys, chunk her down.' And, they said, 'How many times shall we chunk her down, till seven times seven?' And he said, 'Nay, but seventy times seven.' And they chunked her down four hundred and ninety times.

"And she burst asunder in their midst. And they picked up twelve baskets of the leftovers. And, in the resurrection whose wife shall she be?"

The committee chairman suddenly interrupted the young minister's casserole of scriptures and said to the remainder of the committee, "Fellows, I think we ought to ask the church to call him as our minister. He is awfully young, but he sure does know his Bible."

Obviously, the pulpit committee chairperson could have taken his own refresher course in the truths of the Bible.

You can stand on the promises of God; and the greater the stand, the greater the realization of their power.

An elderly man sat on a folding chair on the porch of a local nursing home with his Bible in his lap. Suddenly he shouted, "God is great!"

A ministry intern came over to him and sat in the next chair. "Can't help but hear you talk about God."

"I just read how He parted the waters of the Red Sea and led the Israelites right through," the man said.

"That's right," the intern responded, "I just studied that in Bible school. But did you know that scholars tell us the Red Sea was only about 10 inches deep at the time?"

"Well, that makes Him greater than I thought!" the older man shouted.

"What do you mean?" the intern asked.

The elderly man replied, "He not only led those Israelite folk through the Red Sea, he drowned the enemy in less than a foot of water."

God's Word is true; you can depend on it.

Principle Number 8: The War Is Already Won

It's true that any navigation depends on solid landmarks. That's what Jon Krakauer discovered during a disastrous attempt to climb Mount Everest in May 1996. During that quest to stand upon the 29,028-foot summit, 12 climbers lost their lives. Krakauer was a part of this expedition and has written of the experience in his best-selling book *Into Thin Air.*

Krakauer describes how the imperiled group came to this dreadful fate. On their final ascent to the top, several climbers violated clear instructions to not be on the summit after 2 P.M. This delay caused the entire group to remain in a dangerous sector of the mountain far too long.

A murderous storm blew in on the climbers, and they found

themselves in a fight for their lives. The full-blown blizzard sent the wind-chill factor plummeting 100 degrees below zero. They were enveloped in darkness and blowing snow. Visibility dropped to less than 20 feet. Their oxygen was depleted, and the batteries on their lights faded. For two hours they simply staggered blindly through the snow hoping to stumble upon the camp.

Hypothermia and exhaustion took a terrible toll, and their floundering steps nearly carried them over the precipice of a 7,000-foot cliff. Their search for safety was chaotic.

While the fierce wind continued to create a ground-blizzard, the sky above began to clear. As the climbers looked up, they saw the silhouettes of Everest and Lhotse. From that brief glimpse of these reference points, they were able to determine the route back to camp, safety, and survival.[5]

It's a great truth for the times of your life. God has put some landmarks around to expedite your journey. Some are obvious. And some can only be seen with the eyes of your heart.

1. The Landmark of His Word. Once again, the psalmist David affirms his trust in God's counsel. "Send forth your light and your truth, let them guide me; let them bring me to your holy mountain, to the place where you dwell" (Ps. 43:3).

"Are we there yet?" What parent hasn't gritted his or her teeth a few times when the question repeatedly pops up from the backseat on a long car ride? "Almost," the reply may come. "See that pharmacy on the corner? That means we're almost to Grandpa and Grandma's house."

Landmarks. Scriptural signposts that tell us we're getting close to home—that God's Supernatural Time (GST) has everything on schedule. "When these things begin to take place, stand up and lift up your heads, because your redemption is drawing near" (Luke 21:28).

The frustrating events of time are simply signposts, leading us to a day without frustration—in heaven, seated in glory alongside the saints of all time.

2. The Landmark of His Church. The testimony of ten thousand times ten thousand and thousands of thousands assure us that the times and truths of the Lord are trustworthy. One of the "big events" in heaven will be the reading of the "message board." John the apostle had a Spirit-anointed vision of it. "When he opened the fifth seal, I saw under the altar the souls of those who had been slain because of the word of God and the testimony they had maintained" (Rev. 6:9). The Church—all believers in the Lord Jesus Christ—has put its very life on the line to preach the message of His forgiveness, power, and final victory. And it has posted its message of God's faithfulness.

Some church members on earth have been about as faithful as a food addict in a fajita factory. But the vast majority have trusted and tested the promises of God on the front lines of life and found them to be absolutely true. The halls of heaven will be lined with them.

Granted, sometimes they waited awhile to see promises blossom in their lives—agonizing waits, painful waits. But they came just when they were needed.

The church is a landmark on the way to heaven.

3. The Landmark of His Supply. The apostle James reminded, "Every good and perfect gift is from above, coming down from the Father of the heavenly lights, who does not change like shifting shadows" (James 1:17).

Every earthly benefit is a down payment on the eternal benefits. They're always there—even when you have to search through the scrapbooks of your soul to remember them. That encouraging phone call. That unexpected check in the mail.

The $10.00 you forget you had folded and stuck in your wallet. A part-time job during the holidays.

Accidents? No. The God who promised to supply your need, in His own way and on His own time schedule, appointed them.

4. The Landmark of Your Faith. Why are you trusting God to carry out His wonderful and eternal plans in your life right now? Because you trusted Him before and found Him to be trustworthy. In a letter of encouragement to a young pastor who faced the uncertainties of time and the unsteadiness of his fellow travelers, Paul the apostle reminded Pastor Timothy to watch for the landmarks. "Those who have served well gain an excellent standing and great assurance in their faith in Christ Jesus" (1 Tim. 3:13).

"Timothy," Paul wraps the arms of his heart around the servant of the Lord, "you just hold steady. Your faith is going to pay off in treasures beyond your imagination someday. But in the meantime, keep your hands off the steering wheel. Keep trusting the Lord."

Every baseball fan remembers the 1988 World Series. The Los Angeles Dodgers were playing the Oakland Athletics. The Dodgers' power-hitter, Kirk Gibson, was on the bench with a knee injury.

It was the bottom of the ninth, with two outs. The Dodgers were behind 4-3. There was one runner on base. Kirk Gibson pleaded with manager Tommy Lasorda to let him pinch-hit. Lasorda reluctantly gave in.

Gibson limped up to the plate. Nobody could believe it. The network commentator remarked, "Even if Gibson can hit the ball to the outfield, he'll be thrown out at first base. There's no way he can make it to first on that bad leg."

Quickly, Kirk Gibson was down 0-2 in the count. The next pitch, however, Gibson sent sailing over the fence. A two-run homer that won the game! I'll never forget Gibson pumping his arm and hobbling around the bases. That's a "clutch" hit.

God comes through for us in the clutch. It might be the bottom of the ninth, two outs, down to our last strike—He always comes through just in time.

God's never late.

He's seldom early.

He's always right on time.

---

1. *Houston Chronicle*, 4/1/00, 14A.

2. *Parade*, 12/19/99, 9.

3. Herbert Lockyer, *All the Promises of the Bible*, 1962, 10.

4. Albert Edward Bailey, *The Gospel in Hymns* (New York: Charles Scribner's Sons, 1950), 107-10.

5. Jon Krakauer, *Into Thin Air*, 1997, 278.

About the Author

Stan Toler is senior pastor of Trinity Church of the Nazarene in Oklahoma City, and hosts the television program *Leadership Today.* For the past several years he has taught seminars for Dr. John Maxwell's INJOY Group—a leadership development institute. Toler has written over 50 books, including his best-sellers *God Has Never Failed Me, but He's Sure Scared Me to Death a Few Times*, *The Buzzards Are Circling, but God's Not Finished with Me Yet,* and the popular *Minute Movitators* series.